T0128525

THE LABOUR THAT COUNTS

How Not to Labour in Vain

Femi Lanre-Oke

authorHOUSE®

AuthorHouse™ UK
1663 Liberty Drive
Bloomington, IN 47403 USA
www.authorhouse.co.uk
Phone: 0800.197.4150

King James Version (KJV)
In the public domain.

Scripture quotations marked KJV are from the Holy Bible, King James Version (Authorized Version). First published in 1611. Quoted from the KJV Classic Reference Bible, Copyright © 1983 by The Zondervan Corporation.

Published by AuthorHouse   01/07/2016

ISBN: 978-1-4685-8608-4 (sc)
ISBN: 978-1-4685-8609-1 (e)

Print information available on the last page.

CONTENTS

To the neglected and rejected children of Africa: my heart bleeds for you; may you discover purpose.

To all in search of fulfilment and joy: may this book be of great help.

To all fathers, leaders, and mentors in faith: may your labour count.

To all partners of Jesus Praise Evangelical Ministries International (JPEMI): may your lives speak.

To the source of all life: in you alone we put our trust.

ACKNOWLEDGEMENTS

No one can fulfil destiny in isolation. We all need each other to fulfil all of God's purpose for our lives. I cannot but appreciate all the leaders, fathers, and mentors who directly and indirectly tutored me.

Bishop Francis Wale Oke, I cannot thank you enough; your contribution to my life is immense.

Rev. Olusola Areogun, I appreciate you, sir. His grace and oil be multiplied in Jesus's name.

Pastor J. Babalola of Christ Deliverance Ministries, Pastor Abiodun Emmanuel of the Redeemed Glory Assembly, Prophet Ayo Babalola Akinrinade of Jesus Covenant Revolutional Ministries, Pastor Joe Jacobs of Christ Apostolic Church – you are rare gems, men of worth and substance. This generation is blessed having you at this time.

Mr. Temidayo Akinrinola, my editor, I appreciate you. The Lord will enlarge you.

To all the faithful of Jesus Praise Evangelical Ministries International: may our labour fully count.

To my wife, Olubusola: thanks for standing by me all through my itinerant ministries.

To my parents, the late Elder Joseph and Mrs. Margaret O. Oke, and to Elder and Deacon Wale Farombi: the Lord will continually strengthen you.

To all whose efforts and counsel made this work a reality, who for space I will not be able to mention individually, I say thank you.

INTRODUCTION

Great kudos to all who are labouring day and night to make things work well, especially those labouring in the vineyard of God's kingdom. May you never grow weary.

Interestingly, not all labour will count on the last day. Each person will give account of what he or she has done, and each person will be rewarded according to his or her labour.

The most crucial aspect is that we all want to be rewarded based on what we have done and what is expected of us. The more we have done of what we are meant to do, the more our reward before God. Definitely, not all who are labouring in the vineyard are labouring accordingly.

The apostle Paul said it this way in 1 Corinthians 9:24: 'Know ye not that they which run in a race run all, but one receiveth the prize?' So run, that ye may obtain. Not all who run obtain, so we are encouraged to run so as to obtain. This book is aimed at helping and guiding you to run and obtain.

'And every man that striveth for the mastery is temperate in all things. Now they do it to obtain a corruptible crown; but we are incorruptible' (1 Cor. 9:25).

In this book, you will learn how to discover your purpose in God, recognize your God-given mandates to fulfilling your destiny, and recognize the Enemy's role in fulfilling your roles among other things. I trust God to help you, with the aid of this book, to further run to obtain. I pray that on the last day, when all flesh shall give account of their stewardship, your labour may truly count.

PART I

At the end of this section, you should understand the following:

- your divinely assigned roles
- your potentials
- the God of purpose
- truths about purpose

A life out of order is a life full of chaos. Discovering God's purpose for your life is the first step to recovering self and enjoying life.

—OluwaFemi Lanre-Oke

Experience the joy of self-discovery and open up continents of possibilities in your nature which might otherwise remain undiscovered.

—OluwaFemi Lanre-Oke

1.
UNDERSTANDING YOUR DIVINELY ASSIGNED ROLES

Everything God created is meant to fulfil a particular role; insects, plants, animals, and humans exist to accomplish their preprogrammed tasks.

We all have our roles to play in life. This inspiring book helps us discover our divine roles and maps out modalities to effectively discharge them.

It is a truism that when we do not know why we exist, we malfunction. The intestine in the human body functions only by being in the body – in other words, inside the physical body. If the small intestine fails in its role and takes the role of the large intestine, then death is inevitable, even though they are both intestines. If the arm attempts to become as big as the thigh, then it becomes diseased. If, on the other hand, the thigh reduces in size to match the arm, it too becomes diseased.

Everything is the way it is because it was created to be that way. Our God is a God of purpose, and everything He creates, He does with purpose.

The purpose of a thing is the reason it exists. If purpose is not discovered, existence is not necessary. Fulfilling purpose must be the primary goal of every human being.

All God's creatures are created with purpose in the mind of God. All things begin and end with purpose. Your existence is proof that your generation needs something that you contain.

The chaos we have in life today is a result of our failure to discover and fulfil our roles in life. Every other creation of God lives to fulfil its role to keep things in order – except humans.

Dysfunction in our bodies is often regarded as illness. A disease is a result of certain organs failing to fulfil their roles in the body's system. This failure brings discomfort and pain. The failure of these organs may be facilitated by certain organisms – microorganisms. But the major discomfort is a result of non-performance of the organs. If such organs were alive to their functions, the body would be hale and hearty.

A greater discomfort is unleashed into our world when we fail to recognize our roles or fail to accept them as our fundamental priorities (Col. 4:17). We definitely would give account of our divinely assigned roles to the Lord, but those outside the divinely assigned ones do not count.

The teeth are in the mouth but play a different role from the tongue. Each needs the other's functions for the body to work as a system. The teeth cannot function independently; neither can the tongue. They are dependent on each other.

The world would be a better place to live if each person understood and mastered his or her assigned role.

Our sun is 93 million miles from the earth. If it were 10 million miles nearer, we would burn up. If it were 10 million farther away, we would freeze. The sun is just the correct distance from us to make human life possible. The earth and sun relate to each other purposely so that humanity can exist on the planet.

Other planets are unsuitable for human life. Mercury turns only one side to the sun. One side of the planet is a burning furnace, and the reverse side is a frozen waste. Venus has a dense vapour for atmosphere, making life impossible. Mars has no water, and the temperatures are too low for vegetation or human life.

The earth has a circumference of 25,000 miles. It rotates on its axis once every twenty-four hours, travelling at a speed of approximately one thousand miles per hour. Because it rotates and is not stationary like Mercury, we have day and night. The part of the earth that faces the sun has day and the rest has night. As the earth revolves, night turns to day and day to night.

If the earth revolved at one hundred miles per hour instead of one thousand, then instead of taking twenty-four hours to make one complete revolution, it would take 240 hours. Hence, the day would be ten times longer, such that the heat we experience for twelve hours would extend to 120 hours, burning things up and making life impossible. Nights would likewise be 120 hours long, and this extended dark and cold would freeze things.

Our sun is a source of energy. Its heat is 12,000 degrees. It gives off radiation. If our sun were twice as hot and gave off twice as much radiation, we would burn up; if it were half as hot, we would freeze. So our sun, among millions of other suns, is just right for life on the earth.

The gases we breathe are of just the right mixture and intensity for the preservation of human life. Our atmosphere contains oxygen, nitrogen, argon, neon, and krypton. Nitrogen is 78 per cent and of oxygen is 21 per cent. Oxygen is the breath of life for all land animals and is unobtainable except from the atmosphere. If oxygen were 10 per cent instead of 21 per cent, we could not live. And if it were 50 per cent instead of 21 per cent, all combustible substances in the world would become flammable. The first stroke of lightning to hit a tree would ignite the forest.

Everything is the way it is because of its place in creation.

And when they told *[it]* to Jotham, he went and stood in the top of mount Gerizim, and lifted up his voice, and cried, and said unto them, Hearken unto me, ye men of Shechem, that God may hearken unto you. The trees went forth *[on a time]* to anoint a king over them; and they said unto the olive tree, Reign thou over us. But the olive tree said unto them, Should I leave my fatness, wherewith by me they honour God and man, and go to be promoted over the trees? And the trees said to the fig tree, Come thou, *[and]* reign over us. But the fig tree said unto them, Should I forsake my sweetness, and my good fruit, and go to be promoted over the trees? Then said the trees unto the vine, Come thou, *[and]* reign over us. And the vine said unto them, Should I leave my wine, which cheereth God and man, and go to be promoted over the trees? Then said all the trees unto the bramble, Come thou, *[and]* reign over us. And the bramble said unto the trees, If in truth ye anoint me king over you, *[then]* come *[and]* put your trust in my shadow: and if not, let fire come out of the bramble, and devour the cedars of Lebanon. (Judg. 9:7–15)

2.
UNDERSTANDING YOUR POTENTIAL

Your potential is all you can do that you have not done. It is the ability in you that is yet to be used.

Your potential is not what you have done, but that which you can do that you have not done. It is that idea in you – the book you have not written, the song you have not sung, the research you are about to carry out, the problem you want solved and can solve but have not solved. In life, you will be remembered more for the problems you solved rather than the ones you created.

The potential in you is meant to bring ease to people around you. It is meant to be used to solve existing or likely problems. No problem in life is permitted to exist if it does not have a solution. All problems are seen as problems because humanity has failed to discover its roles. Everything that God created is meant to solve a particular problem. If God has called you to do certain work, it is because you have been equipped with whatever you will need to do it. God will not and does not call His people to do what He has not equipped them to do.

Our world contains men and women with unfulfilled dreams because they are conscious only of the circumstances surrounding them and not of the revelation of their identities – who they are, the innate potential they carry, and the special abilities they have as the image of the omnipotent God – the all-potential God.

Work is the major key that unlocks potentials within us, not dreams and wishes.

Potential is given to us because of the assignment that has been committed to our trust. In other words, we are the way we are because of the reason behind our existence. This is crucial to discovering our roles in life and fulfilling them.

We must understand that our life components are made up of the materials and gifts that best fit our assignments in life. Nobody born of a woman on this earth is a mistake. We may have illegal parents but not illegal children, irrespective of the circumstances surrounding birth. Anyone born into this world has an equal chance of making it and breaking forth in the area of his or her calling.

We all have been wired in a way that will facilitate our existence. We are all products of the Divine Maker; our existence is not by accident. We are made in His image and likeness and have been called by God to play certain roles for which we have been equipped. It is the discovery of such roles that makes life really meaningful and fruitful.

Our potential is God's gift and part of the God's divine provision to help us fulfil these roles. However, this potential can be unlocked only through work and a strong aversion to idleness.

'The greatest thing a man can do in this world,' said Dr Orison Swett Marden, 'is to make the most possible out of the stuff that has been given him. This is success, and there is no other.' H. W. Shaw said, 'The greatest thief this world has ever produced is procrastination, and he is still at large.'

Dr Sidney Bremer wrote, 'On the great clock of time there is but one word – *now!* To attain successful achievement you must be a man or woman of action! There is no other way. When your goal is made, when your sail is set, you must act at once.'

'Outside of man there is not an idle atom in the universe; everything is working out its mission,' wrote Marden. "'Work is the one great law of the world," said Zola, "which leads organized matter slowly but steadily to its own goal. It is a law of nature that the moment activity ceases anywhere, there a retrograde process sets in."'

'Work or starve' is nature's motto, and God's counsel is that, when you become all you were meant to be, it is then that you give God glory.

For I am now ready to be offered, and the time of my departure is at hand. I have fought a good fight, I have finished *[my]* course, I have kept the faith: Henceforth there is laid up for me a crown of righteousness, which the Lord, the righteous judge, shall give me at that day: and not to me only, but unto all them also that love his appearing. (2 Tim. 4:6–8)

3.
UNDERSTANDING THE GOD OF PURPOSE

Everything created by God exists for a unique purpose. God is not the God of a fun fair who has nothing to do and hence plays around with things. God in His greatness created the heavens and the earth for specific reasons. He created all the inhabitants for good reasons.

The truth is that life is unfulfilling and frustrating when God's purpose is unknown. The most tragic thing in life is the inability to discover one's reason for existence. Fulfilment is unrealistic without understanding the nature of purpose.

Purpose is the intent for which something is created. It is the reason that you exist. Purpose is the reason that anything exists. It is the reason that God created you. The discovery of purpose is the discovery of the role a man or woman is to fulfil on earth.

The truth about purpose includes the following statements:

- The human need for personal satisfaction is universal.
- Personal fulfilment is the only true measure for success.
- Fulfilling a purpose must be the primary goal for every person.
- Everything in life has a purpose.
- Purpose is the original intent in the mind of the Creator that motivates Him to create a particular thing.
- Purpose always precedes production.
- All things begin and end with purpose.
- God created you with a purpose in mind.
- Purpose is inherent.
- Purpose is individual – you are the way you are because of why you are.
- Purpose can be multiple.
- Purpose is interdependent – purpose can't be fulfilled in isolation.
- Purpose is permanent.
- Purpose is resilient. God's purpose for your life cannot be reversed by your past.
- Purpose is universal.

The principle of purpose includes the following statements:

- God is a God of purpose – everything God created is for a purpose.
- Everything in life has a purpose.
- Ignorance of purpose does not cancel purpose.
- Not every purpose is known.
- Whenever and wherever purpose is not known, abnormal use (abuse) is inevitable.
- To know the purpose of a thing, never ask the thing.
- Purpose is known only in the mind of the Creator.
- Purpose is the key to fulfilment.
- Your design is unique. You are the way you are because of the why you are.

PART II

At the end of this section, you should understand the following:

- your roles in life
- the different kinds of roles
  - roles in ministry
  - roles in governance
  - roles in family

He who spends more time with man than with God will do less for man and for God.
—OluwaFemi Lanre-Oke

He who prays less will do more to achieve less.
—OluwaFemi Lanre-Oke

4.
DISCOVERING YOUR ROLES IN LIFE

The ultimate in the mind of God is that we discover what He has designed us for and we accomplish it. As humans, we are not meant to design but to discover what is designed. So many people are playing other people's roles, either because they have not found their own roles or have not yielded to God's arrangement for their lives.

Most people don't accept their roles because they prefer other people's roles to their divinely programmed ones. So they suffer and are frustrated on earth, doing what they have not been equipped to do. Nothing can be more frustrating than this. It's like making furrows not with a hoe, but rather with a cutlass. God does not make provision for any arrangement He has not preprogrammed.

We must watch what we are doing to be sure it is what we are supposed to do. Parents should not force their children to live their unfulfilled dreams. Children must be allowed to live their own dreams. A father, for instance, who desired to be an engineer and could not, might wish to compel his child to do such a course against the will of the child. This is improper, and it frustrates the joy of the child.

In discovering our roles in life, certain key factors can be of help.

Seeking God to Find your Role

This is absolute and total. To find the purpose of a thing, you do not ask the thing. A chair cannot tell its purpose; the purpose can be known only in the mind of the maker. Every manufacturer naturally will accompany its product with a manual to guide the customer in the usage of the product.

Nobody knows a product better than the person who makes it. You cannot know a Toyota car like those who made the car. No prophet knows you as well as God does. Other people may have an idea of who you are, but their ideas may be misconceptions. Your true image and identity can be found only in God. Knowing God is the first step in knowing your identity, potential, and role in life.

No one can know the Father except as He is revealed to him or her. Coming to church or being busy with church activities is not a yardstick in determining if you know God or not.

Many people come to church regularly. Some are born in the church. Some are leaders of a unit in the church. Yet these people may not know God. Even if they claim to know God, He may not know them as His own.

You might be different. You may be the type who does not even go to church or regard the teachings of God as valuable. Life cannot be meaningful outside the One who made it. The reason there is emptiness in your life, despite your struggle and your achievement, is that the Creator's place in your life has been taken over by another thing that cannot perform the role the way the Creator can. This thing could relate to money, lust, fellowship, friendship, or church activity. No matter what it is, it is the wrong thing. Only one thing is needful, and that is staying with Jesus Christ.

If you want God to take His place in your life and play His role in your journey to fulfilment, the step to take is simple. Right away, confess all your sins to God. Ask the Lord to forgive you and to cleanse you with His blood that was shed for you on the cross of Calvary.

Confess now that Jesus Christ is the Son of God, and that He died for your sins. Tell God to take your life of sins for the sake of His Son, Jesus, and give you His life in Jesus's name. Amen.

Now you are saved. Make sure you keep a good fellowship with the Lord and His Word. Do not forsake the company of godly brethren. In other words, find a gospel church and attend. You will surely flourish.

Having been recognized by God by being saved, learn to talk and fellowship with God. Ask Him to show you what His plans and purpose for your life are.

Tell God to speak to you concerning your roles in life, and sincerely He will surely do so. Do not limit God to a particular channel of communication. God can speak to you in many ways:

- *Through His Word* – His Word is settled in heaven and earth either through your meditation on scripture or through an explanation of a character in scripture or by instructing you to study a particular aspect of scripture. His Word will surely guide you.

- *Through intuition* – God can speak to your spirit, and your spirit can communicate to your mind the desires of God for your life.
- *Through the Holy Spirit* – The Holy Spirit can speak to your ears and your heart. It might be an audible voice of God talking to you about His will and counsel for you.
- *Through a night vision* – God can speak to you in a vision about His plan and counsel for your life.
- *Through revelation* – God can reveal to you details of His will and counsel.
- *Through strong desire* – At times God's will can be communicated to humans through a strong desire to do God's will; such desire can be judged by scripture before one acts upon it.
- *Through prophecies* – God's mind and counsel are often revealed through godly inspirational prophecies.
- *Through dreams* – Dreams at times are God's channel of communicating His will and counsel to His people.

Other Ways to Find your Role

Apart from seeking God to know your role, you can also gain insight by observing:

- *What you hate* – What do you really hate that happens to people and that you know does not please God? That thing you hate happening to others – because it hurts them and it does not please God – is a problem you are called to solve.
- *What irritates you* – This is similar to the first one. What are the things that irritate you and get you angry? I mean angry because such things do not benefit humanity and do not glorify God. They are indicators of what you are to correct.
- *What problems you easily find or discover* – What are the problems you can easily locate that others do not find? Sometimes a person can get into a place and see a problem with the colour combination of the decoration of the room. This may not be observed by others. The problems we easily identify that others do not see are problems we have been wired to solve.

- *What you enjoy doing* – These are the things that gladden your heart when you do them. I mean positive things: for example, when you help others, counsel them, teach them, give to them. Whatever you enjoy doing to help humanity or your society may be a pointer to what you are called to do.

- *What you can do with ease* – We each have different abilities and skills. Our potential is what it is because of the reason behind our existence. There are certain things we can do very well, not necessarily because of specialized training but simply because the ability is inbuilt. Things we can do with ease are indications of what we have been called to do.

- *Whom we walk with* – It is a common saying: 'Show me your friends and I will tell you who you are.' As a mirror reflects the face of a person, so does a friend reflect one's soul. The people you walk with have something in common with you. I often tell people around me that if you have nine friends and eight of them are pastors, then you are surely one. There is something about friendship that reflects who a person is. The people you hang around with or walk with determine who you are

- *Whom you enjoy listening to* – These are the people you love to hear. They are people who carry what you need and, in essence, reveal what you need. They in one way reflect your identity. No matter what field these people are in and no matter their background, if you are used to listening to them and enjoy it, they are reflectors of what you carry.

- *Whom you love to be like* – The people you admire influence your life. These people are your mentors and role models, irrespective of their field. You love their contributions to society and you are thrilled by their achievements. Such men and women may be your role models. You naturally admire them and desire to be like them. They are great indicators of the things in you.

- *What potential within you seeks expression* – There are times when you feel your abilities are seeking expression. You desire to be given an opportunity to do something you believe you will do well even when you have not done it before. The way it is being done irritates you, and there is a conviction within you that you can do it better. You feel cheated when denied the opportunity to bring this potential to expression. You may not know how to put the feeling into words. You know only that there is an invisible hand beckoning you to fulfil destiny. You know there is something in you that, if realized, will better the lot of others. That thing in you seeking expression, when well trained, becomes a tool in the hands of God to bless the world. That thing is an indication of what you are called to do.

- *What books you enjoy reading* – Books are the written convictions of people about issues around them. The authors you love to read or the titles of books that catch your attention are indications of what is in you.

- *What makes you laugh* – What makes you laugh and be glad when you do it, especially when it helps humanity and glorifies God, reflects what is within you.

- *What makes you cry* – What draws tears from your eyes because it humiliates humanity and does not glorify God is what you are to correct.

5.
THE DIFFERENT KINDS OF ROLES

Each human being has one role or another to play in life. The great challenge is that not all have discovered their roles. Those who have discovered theirs have not all accepted them. Some prefer the roles of others to their own. And among those who have accepted their roles are people who have yet to heed the instructions therein. Even if some of them heed the instructions, few of them are at the threshold of fulfilling their purpose.

We all have roles to play in life, either positive or negative. Pharaoh was designed by God to play a negative role. Herod played a negative role. Judas Iscariot played a negative role. There are many others. My prayer is that your name will not be counted among those who will play negative roles in life in Jesus's name.

For the purpose of this book, I shall discuss three kinds of roles from which every other role emanates. These three kinds of roles are related to three kinds of calling. They are roles in ministry, roles in governance, and roles in family.

6.
ROLES IN MINISTRY

The first roles I will discuss are roles in ministry. Many people are given major and specific roles in the ministry.

Most of the people we read about in the Bible are men and women who played significant roles in the counsel of God at that particular time on earth. It was not as though the people we read about in the Bible were the only people on the earth at that time; however, they were the people who were relevant to what God was doing in their time.

Likewise today, if we would be relevant in our generation, we must learn to cooperate with God's will and counsel. To be relevant, we must be part of what God is doing in our time.

And he gave some, apostles; and some, prophets; and some, evangelists; and some, pastors and teachers; For the perfecting of the saints, for the work of the ministry, for the edifying of the body of Christ: Till we all come in the unity of the faith, and of the knowledge of the Son of God, unto a perfect man, unto the measure of the stature of the fulness of Christ. (Eph. 4:11–13)

As the apostles (Christ's envoys) govern the church, and the prophets (Christ's channels of *rhema* and *apocalypses*) guide, the evangelists (Christ's magnetizers) gather or bring people into the body of Christ. The pastors (Christ's under-shepherds) guard their sheep by feeding, nurturing, and protecting from enemies. The teachers ensure that the body of Christ is well grounded in the knowledge of God.

These five gifts are referred to as *ministerial* or *office* gifts – or, better put, gifts of God the Son.

Now there are diversities of gifts, but the same Spirit. And there are differences of administrations, but the same Lord. And there are diversities of operations, but it is the same God which worketh all in all. (1 Cor. 12:4–6)

And God hath set some in the church, first apostles, secondarily prophets, thirdly teachers, after that miracles, then gifts of healings, helps, governments, diversities of tongues. (1 Cor. 12:28)

For as we have many members in one body, and all members have not the same office: So we, *[being]* many, are one body in Christ, and every one members one of another. Having then gifts differing according to the grace that is given to us, whether prophecy, *[let us prophesy]* according to the proportion of faith; Or ministry, *[let us wait]* on *[our]* ministering: or he that teacheth, on teaching; Or he that exhorteth, on exhortation: he that giveth, *[let him do it]* with simplicity; he that ruleth, with diligence; he that sheweth mercy, with cheerfulness. (Rom. 12:4–8)

Though I speak with the tongues of men and of angels, and have not charity, I am become *[as]* sounding brass, or a tinkling cymbal. And though I have *[the gift of]* prophecy, and understand all mysteries, and all knowledge; and though I have all faith, so that I could remove mountains, and have not charity, I am nothing. And though I bestow all my goods to feed *[the poor]*, and though I give my body to be burned, and have not charity, it profiteth me nothing. (1 Cor. 13:1–3)

The gifts of God the Son are roles as the coaches for others. They equip the saint for work in the ministry and to edify the body of Christ. They train others to effectively fulfil their roles on earth.

Apart from the five office gifts of God the Son, we have the gifts of God the Father, also known as motivational or creational gifts. These include the roles of the motivator, servant, exorcist, exhorter, generous giver, hospitable one, missionary, merciful one, helper, celibate, leader, administrator, martyr, and volunteer for poverty.

Apostles

Apostles are referred to as the *sent ones*. They are God's messengers sent forth to pioneer and establish new works. The word *apostle* (Greek *apostolos*) simply means messenger. Apostles are the people sent out to deliver the message of Christ to others.

The ministerial gift of apostles is the divine ability, severally and graciously bestowed on certain members of the body of Christ, to assume and exercise general leadership over a large number of churches. Apostles have a unique authority in spiritual matters, which is spontaneously recognized and appreciated by those churches.

More than twelve apostles were mentioned in the New Testament. Apostles are specially equipped to establish churches in places where the good news has never been proclaimed. This they accomplish with divine ease. They have spiritual authority that cuts across cultures, languages, denominations, and religions. They are given 'keys to the kingdom' to open the door of faith to the world (Matt. 6:19).

Apostles do extensive evangelism and mission, plant churches, train faithful brethren, pray for them, ordain them, and commit these churches into their hands. With divine knowledge, wisdom, and leadership, apostles plan, coordinate, and control the activities of these churches.

There are other, modern terms for apostles, depending on the administrative system of each church organization, such as president, general overseer, or bishop. These describe the function of an apostle by office. Some people today are not apostles by calling, yet they occupy the office of an apostle.

Christ Jesus gives apostles the authority to govern the church. Apostles have almost all the spiritual gifts. They have a transparent holiness, exemplary humility, and often the grace to do outstanding miracles, signs, and wonders. Most importantly, they have the zeal to cover the world with the gospel.

Interestingly, God calls people today not only as apostles in ministry but also in governance. For example, there are people sent forth to bring major changes to the political and economic realms of a nation through apostolic mandate and calling.

Apostles must not see themselves as people who have it all or know it all and hence idolize themselves to be served and worshipped. Rather, apostles must see themselves as sent by God to fulfil a particular mission for which they will be held accountable.

The perfect type of the apostle is in the New Testament. He is known as the Apostle and High Priest of our faith, the Lord Jesus Himself. Jesus came as the original prototype for all apostles.

Aside from Jesus, there are four types of apostles. Let's look at each type and see what their role is.

The Moses Apostolic Type

Jesus was the fulfilment of Moses' prophecy. Jesus was another Moses in terms of scripture. Jesus came in the spirit of Moses. He came in the ministry of Moses – to do what? To do the same thing that Moses did – to deliver the people from their bondage.

However, they misunderstood Him. They thought He was coming to deliver them from the Romans. They didn't realize that their bondage to sin was far greater than their bondage to Rome. He came to deliver them from their bondage to sin, from their bondage to Satan, and all they could see was the more obvious external oppression. Why? Because Israel was still living in "types" and shadows. They were still living in the physical Promised Land that had been promised to them.

Jesus came to bring them to the true Promised Land. They thought they were going to get back the land of Israel. But Jesus came to bring them a life of blessing, a life that flowed with milk and honey, not just in the physical realm but in the spiritual as well. They misunderstood His purpose, but He did accomplish it.

Jesus came to show them God in a new and wonderful way. He came to fulfil the same functions as Moses. He came to give them direction and counsel.

Do you remember poor old Moses standing there all day while the people gathered and came to him one at a time? I have been there. Everybody wants a time of prayer. Everybody wants personal ministry. Everybody thinks that he or she is the most important person in the world, and if you spend five hours with him or her ... well, everybody else can wait.

Jesus came to teach the people how to hear from God. He did not come to be there to meet their needs. He brought the revelation of God to them. He brought an opportunity for them to reach out and touch God themselves. But they made the same mistake. Jesus was Moses all over again, but with a new spiritual emphasis. Can you see the picture?

The Moses type of apostle directs ministry largely at the status quo church. The status quo is what everybody does. It is the 'in thing'. It is the fashion of this world. The status quo church is a church that is following the patterns of this world, that has become absorbed and controlled by the world. It is a church that is behaving just like the world.

The status quo church is no different to any worldly organization. It has become a business, a club. It has been absorbed into the world system. The Moses type of apostle is called primarily to address that aspect of the church, to deal with it and to break the church free. Why? Because Moses was called to deliver the Israelites out of Egypt. They cried to be delivered – until they had to leave behind all the good things in their lives as well as the bad things.

The Moses apostle has a big job on his hands. How is he going to do it? He is going to do it in the same way Moses delivered the children of Israel from Egypt.

The Moses apostle introduces the church to the correct pattern. God gave Moses the pattern for the tabernacle. He was very fussy about how it should be done, and very exact about how it should be set up.

You say, 'But we already have a pattern for the church. The church is doing well, thank you very much.'

Yes, but the church is living in Egypt. They are doing well there. Do you want to carry on living in that house? Do you want to have the same work hours and the same pay?

You say, 'But our pattern is working fine.'

Yes, it is working great – under slavery. There has to be a new pattern. There must be a change in the way things are being done in the church. God has called Moses to stand up and say, 'That is the wrong way. This is the right way. This is the way you have to do it. You must stop doing that, and you must start doing this. You've got to cut that out.'

Moses brings God back into the old structures by changing them. He brings about a change in the system. He addresses the status quo. His entire motivation and task is to change the mindsets of the people to a form that God can work in.

Moses will show the people the way to the Promised Land. What is the Promised Land? The Promised Land is the life of blessing that God has for us.

Have you ever heard of the way of blessing? It is about as close to Moses as you get. It shows the people how to find the Promised Land. The way is hidden. You have to go through a special, secret pass in the mountains to get there.

Moses has been there. He knows the way. Moses is going to show God's people how to enter into all that God has for them. Moses is going to give them the principles and teach them everything that they need to know, and then his job is done.

Jesus was more than that. In Revelation 22:16, He says, 'I, Jesus, have sent mine angel to testify to you these things in the churches. I am the root and the offspring of David, and the bright and morning star.'

He was the root and the offspring of David. What was one of the most common titles that Jesus was known by as He walked the earth? 'Jesus, you son of David, have mercy on me!' (Luke 18:38).

Jesus came as a David. He came to restore the throne of David. The Jews thought He was going to kick Herod out and take over. They missed it again! They were thinking in natural terms. He came to show them how they could reign in life through His power. He came as a new, spiritual David. He came to be the anti-type, but they were still living in the type and the shadow of the old covenant.

Now we are beginning to see a picture of a type and shadow in the ministries of Moses and

David in the Old Testament, from which the whole apostolic function is derived.

What comes next? It is naturally the David type of apostle. What did David do?

The David Apostolic Type

The David apostolic type directs ministry largely to those who have already left the system or the status quo church. They have become fed up. They have had enough and said, 'We're out of here.' Or they received the left boot of fellowship. They have been kicked out. They claim that they want nothing to do with the system, but usually the truth is that the system wants nothing to do with them. Either way, they have left. They are a bunch of dropouts. Nobody wants them. They are considered losers.

They live in the Cave of Adullam, and that is where the David apostle gathers them. He brings them outside of the system. He ministers to them and builds them up. He shows them a pattern of what God has for them.

David does far more than that, though. David apostles bring the church to a place of blessing and prosperity. David's goal was to bring the land of Israel into unity, peace, and a place of security. I have bad news for you if you are a David, though. You have the same problem as Moses. You are not going to finish the job. Somebody else is going to do it.

The David apostle removes traditions and brings the church into contact with the living God. David says, 'I'm just going to go and get the ark.' He is so sick of tradition that he swings the pendulum and overdoes it the other way.

How do I know this? God gave Moses very clear instructions on how the ark of the covenant was to be transferred. It was to be carried by the priests on poles with a curtain covering it. We read how the ark of the covenant was captured by the Philistines and then returned and kept in the house of Obed-Edom.

David said, 'We've got to bring the ark back. We have to bring the glory of God back again. We must bring the presence of God back again!'

The traditional way to move the ark was to send four priests to do it with a couple of sticks. David didn't like this. He was modern. He said, 'We're not going to do it the traditional way. That's the way the old people did it. We're doing it a new way now. We'll get a special, brand-new ox cart, the latest Mercedes model. We will put the ark of the covenant on "the best" and bring it back in glory.'

You know the story of what happened when they tried that. Poor old Uzzah tried to protect the ark, and God killed him. All Uzzah wanted to do was to stop it from falling!

God was saying to David in no uncertain terms, 'David, you do it my way!'

David eventually brought the ark back, but he still didn't follow tradition. He did put the ark behind curtains in a tent, as it had been in the tabernacle of Moses. The difference was that the tent was wide open. It was just a simple little tent right there in his home, a place where people could come. He raised up singers and musicians to praise and worship God, which had not been done in the tabernacle of Moses.

He introduced a new element, a fresh dimension. He introduced a new life into worship – coming into the presence of God with far greater glory than there had been before. David brought an atmosphere that was not traditional. He did away with some of the old ways of doing things and brought new elements into the church.

That is what a David apostle is going to do. He is going to bring a new freshness, a new presence of God, and a new awareness of God's glory and power. He is going to reject the old way of doing things. He is going to say, 'The old pattern is all wrong.'

A David apostle doesn't have much choice in that, because if he did it the old way, everybody following him would desert him. The only reason they come to him is that they have been rejected by the traditional system. They want something new and fresh.

Moses prepared the people in the system for change. David prepared the people outside of the system to get back into a pattern. Each of them was preparing the church of God for the final manifestation of what God will bring His end-times church. Each of them was called only to prepare the church. They will not lead the church into God's final plan.

You say, 'Oh dear, and I was so looking forward to being a David!'

What then remains? Jesus came as Moses and as David, but the work of Jesus was not done yet. There was more to come. There were two who followed Moses and David. There were two who were discipled by Moses and David and who received the baton as it was passed on to them. They were the ones who brought to pass what Moses and David had prepared the people for.

In the same way, the Moses apostle and the David apostle will prepare the church for the final move of God, but those who lead the church into the experience of that final move will not be Moses and David. They will be Joshua and Solomon.

The Joshua Apostolic Type

Joshua was Moses' disciple. The Joshua apostle is zealous for the principles introduced by Moses.

When God told Moses to appoint seventy elders so God could put an anointing upon them, two elders failed to turn up. The anointing of God came down on the sixty-eight who had gone to the meeting place. The power of God also came upon the two who remained in the camp, and they began to prophesy.

Joshua turned to Moses and said, 'My lord, shut them up. They can't do this! That's out of order. It's contrary to what you said. Sort them out!'

Joshua was ready to defend Moses. He actually was Moses' bodyguard. His main function was to protect Moses.

The Joshua apostle takes over where the Moses apostle leaves off and completes the work. It was not Moses who led the Israelites into the land of Canaan and gave it to them; rather, it was Joshua.

The Joshua apostle displaces the system. Joshua went into the land and drove the enemy off so that the Promised Land could be inhabited by the Israelites. The Joshua apostle hands over the church to a new generation. Not one of those who left Egypt made it into Canaan except Joshua and Caleb. The church of tomorrow will be led by a new generation, and the old will die out.

Finally, the Joshua apostle brings rest to the body of Christ. 'And the LORD gave them rest round about, according to all that he sware unto their fathers: and there stood not a man of all their enemies before them; the LORD delivered all their enemies into their hand' (Josh. 21:44).

Joshua gave the Israelites the land. He conquered it and divided it and handed it over to them. It is said that they finally had rest from their enemies.

The Solomon Apostolic Type

And so we come to the final apostolic type – the Solomon apostle. Solomon was discipled by his father, David. Solomon was zealous to enact change according to David's pattern. David introduced a new concept to those who had left the system; Solomon set up and put in place the pattern that David had introduced.

The Solomon apostle brings an emphasis on love, not war. Joshua was the warrior. With him was big strife and conflict. His war cries were, 'Go kill him! Rout the system! Destroy it! Push it out!'

Solomon waited for David to battle through all the warfare. Then Solomon settled down and became a gentleman. He entered into the prosperity that David had prepared the people for. Solomon brings an emphasis on working smart, not hard. Solomon brings wisdom. He brings the right way of doing things. Solomon waits for all the fighting to blow over and says, 'Okay, guys, we're going to build from scratch. Let me show you how to do it the right way.'

Solomon comes with wisdom, with the right pattern and the right principles, and he has no opposition, because he is building on new ground.

He doesn't have to go into the status quo. He builds a new church, something that replaces the system.

Solomon brings the power of God to the people. 'And it came to pass, when the priests were come out of the holy *[place]*, that the cloud filled the house of the LORD, So that the priests could not stand to minister because of the cloud: for the glory of the LORD had filled the house of the LORD' (1 Kgs 8:10–11). That is a description of what happened as Solomon completed the building of the temple. Who made the plans? David did. Who supplied the finance? David did. You say, 'Solomon was such a brilliant guy. He made so much money.' You could too, if you started out as a millionaire! Solomon just used wisely what was handed over to him on a platter. It was given to him.

The Solomon apostle moves in the glory. When he puts the church in place in accordance with the correct pattern, God's glory comes down. The people cannot stand because the glory cloud of God comes down. Everybody falls flat on their faces, falling under the power of God.

God is raising up His end-times apostles – the four different types. What are they going to do? They are going to restore the church to God's correct order and prepare the bride for the return of the Bridegroom. To do this, God is raising up people who will function like Moses, David, Joshua, or Solomon. Where do you stand in this plan?

Prophets

The fact that today we have false prophets — prophets who are not sent by God to deliver a particular message, but who send themselves or are sent by the Devil — is an indication that there are genuine prophets. Today, just as there were prophets of God in the Old Testament, we have prophets of God in the new dispensation.

Prophets of God are most appropriately regarded as the messengers of the Lord. They are God's mouthpieces, and they speak for God when God inspires them to. Without fear or favour of man, the prophets speak the whole truth as they have received it from the Lord. Prophets most times have abilities to understand and interpret accurately symbolic dreams.

Prophets receive revelations from God in the form of visions and dreams. They operate in the gifts of knowledge, wisdom, and discernment of spirit.

Every called preacher has some level of prophetic ability, but not every preacher is a prophet by office. The word *prophet* or *prophetess* is from the Greek words *pro* and *phemi* or *prophemi*, which means 'to speak forth'. To foretell means to speak the truth as received from the Lord.

A true prophet of the Lord does not speak because he or she feels like speaking, but speaks as the Lord gives utterance, without fear or prejudice.

A person may have a gift of prophecy, but that does not mean that the person is a prophet or prophetess. The gift of prophecy is a divine ability that God gives to some members of the body of Christ so that they can receive and communicate a message from God through a divinely anointed utterance. This kind of utterance is also called *unction*. Prophecy, one of the revelation gifts, can come in the form of a special tongue. It becomes a prophecy when it is accurately interpreted.

In some very concrete situations, a prophet reveals the true will of God to the people. This may be encouragement, warning, glorious promises, or comfort.

God uses the prophet to monitor and guide His people, especially in their social, moral, and spiritual endeavours. The prophetic gift and calling is not meant to extort others, to cheat others, or to claim their material and financial resources. Men may give a prophet of their substance of their own will, but a prophet must not build on the prophetic grace to extort others. A prophet will surely give account of his or her stewardship.

The following attributes are indicators that define those who have been called into the prophetic office:

- Prophets must have the conviction. People must notice this, and the local church must attest to the fact that a person has been called into the prophetic office.
- Genuine prophets are never 'parrots'. They talk very sparingly. They are eloquent mostly when revealing the will of God to man, for now or the future.
- The prophet of God must have some measure of asceticism or self-denial. He or she must be given to fasting and prayer.

- Prophets of God have an iron smile; they teach with boldness, talk authoritatively, and are fearless preachers.
- Constant dreams, visions, and trances that come to pass literally in the physical realm characterize a true prophet.
- Prophetic unction (immediate words of supernatural origin), knowledge, and understanding of the spiritual are characteristic of prophets.
- Most prophets are versed in the Word of God, and they have their followers. Every good Christian leader has some measure of prophetic treasure.
- Prophets command the respect of all, though they may be hated by some people. People are curious to hear a prophet's predictions.
- Most prophets also have the gifts of mixed tongues, interpretation of tongues, discernment, faith, healing, and martyrdom.
- Prophetic calling is filled with miracles. People follow the prophet not only because he or she makes God's will known to

them by foretelling, but because of the miraculous.

- A genuine prophet of God is devoid of moral decadence and holds holiness in highest esteem.
- The crowning prophetic indicator is fulfilment of predictions. Fulfilled prophecy is the sign of the authenticity of a prophet (Deut. 18:21–22; 1 Sam. 9:6). Such prophecy must also agree with the written Word of God.

All these indicators may not appear simultaneously, but most of them are bound to manifest in anyone called into the prophetic office. Just as the device is pushing uncalled people (those not called by God into the prophetic office) into establishing themselves as prophets, it has prevented countless called prophets from seeing themselves as prophets of God.

This is one reason why you must prayerfully discover, develop, and deploy God's gifts in your life. To be effective as God's prophet, you must understand the meaning and application of (a) divine revelations, (b) divine interpretation of divine revelations, and (c) the right application of the interpretation.

A prophet of God one day saw a man close to him and prophetically saw musical notes all over him. He called the man and told him that God had just spoken to the prophet to say that the man knew how to play musical instruments very well. The man replied that he did not know how to play musical notes. The prophet insisted on God's revelation.

It was true that God had shown the prophet the revelation, but the true interpretation was that the man owned a store where he sold musical instruments.

Identifying the Signs of Prophetic Calling

If you are called to be a prophet, then you are likely to see a fair portion of the following signs in your life and experience. Some of these signs apply to any major calling to the ministry. Some signs are specific to the prophetic ministry.

The first sign of your prophetic calling is that a desire has been burning in you for a long time to minister to the body of Christ. This is not a passing fancy. It is not so much a desire to bring unbelievers to know the Lord, but more a desire to help believers in their daily walk. It might be a desire to warn people of certain dangers. It might be a desire to encourage and lift believers up. Whichever direction it takes, this thing has taken hold of you and will not let go.

The call of God comes from God and not you. All you can produce in yourself is sin. Paul says, 'For I know that in me (that is, in my flesh,) dwelleth no good thing: for to will is present with me; but *[how]* to perform that which is good I find not' (Rom. 7:18).

The desire to do the work of God is planted by God and grows over a period of time. If you desire to do something for God's glory, then the desire must have come from Him. If it does not fade over time, then it is not an emotional fantasy but something real. If you can identify with this, then mark it as the first sign of your prophetic calling.

The second sign of prophetic calling is that not many people are likely to share your enthusiasm for what you want to do. They may warn you to be careful, to calm down. They might even accuse you of being paranoid. They might tell you not to 'rock the boat'. You may begin to wonder if this thing is of the Lord.

Your ministry is unique, so do not expect others to share your burden. The fact that you want to do something different could be proof that this desire is from the Lord. The Lord tends to hide His prophets away until they are ready. So do not expect others to quickly recognize your call unless you have ministered to them personally. If you have been rejected, ostracized, or accused of going against the general flow, then there is a good chance that the early signs of a prophetic calling have started to show.

The third sign of prophetic calling is that your desire is other oriented. You are not so much concerned with making a name for yourself as you are with helping other people. You will gladly give up things that are important to you so that other people may benefit from your actions. The prophetic ministry, like the apostolic ministry, requires a total commitment to the work of the Lord.

Ministry is servanthood and is likely to cost you a lot. If your desire is not to help others, then you do not have a calling to ministry. Jesus said, 'And whoever will be chief among you, let him be your servant: Even as the Son of man came not to be ministered unto, but to minister, and to give his life a ransom for many' (Matt. 20:27–28).

You must be prepared to pay the price before you can take up your calling. If your desire is not for the good of others, you have not yet even entered the door.

The fourth sign of prophetic calling is that over a period of time, you have found yourself ministering to a particular area of need more than others. It seems that you always end up ministering to believers who need encouragement and direction in their lives. And when you do, something happens inside you, and you sense a surge taking place. You may find yourself telling people which way they should go and what God's purpose is for them.

The Lord prepares you for ministry by creating opportunities for you. Often you will not be aware of this. You know only that you feel content ministering to believers and helping them to set their lives and ministries in order. These are all signs showing you the way to your prophetic calling.

The fifth sign of prophetic calling is that people have told you that you have helped them, even when at times you have not been aware of it. Sometimes others can see your ministry more clearly than you can see it yourself. Solomon said, 'A man's gift makes room for him, And bringeth him before great men' (Prov. 18:16). If you have a prophetic calling, you will not be able to hide it indefinitely. It will show itself in time, and others will notice it.

The sixth sign of prophetic calling is that you feel unqualified to do the work of the Lord. You usually feel unworthy to push yourself forward to suggest that you be given an opportunity. When appeals are made for help, you wait for everyone else to step forward first before you offer your services.

Humility is a sure sign of your genuineness. The Spirit of God always leads gently. He is likened to a dove that is meek and easily frightened away. Jesus is called the Lamb of God. A lamb is also a gentle creature that does not push its way. Since the call comes gently, you may wonder at times if you have heard rightly.

The seventh sign of prophetic calling is a leading to intercessory prayer. If you find yourself being led to spend a lot of time interceding for others, and you have seen definite results, the elements of a prophetic ministry are certainly there. The prophet is the key to what God does in the earth. God said in the Old Testament that He does nothing unless He first reveals His secret to the prophets. If you have been led to pray things into existence or birth them in the Spirit through intercessory prayer, then your prophetic ministry is already starting to manifest.

The eighth sign of prophetic calling is sensitivity to the moving of God's Spirit. A prophet has the ability to bring anointing into a meeting. This is often seen in musical capability or effective leadership in praise and worship. If you have been effectively involved in leading the congregation and can cause the anointing of the Spirit to come upon a group when you lead, this can certainly be very clear sign of a prophetic calling in operation.

The ninth sign of prophetic calling is that your preparation will span many years and will be one a difficult and troublesome process. Prophets are battered and broken and brought to nothing in themselves before they can be of any use to the kingdom of God. They learn to trust not in themselves or in their own abilities. Their knowledge and natural strengths are tried in the fire and brought to naught before God uses them as prophets.

If your life has been one of intense problems, failures, oppositions, persecutions, and pressure, then this could be a sign of preparation for the prophetic ministry. I have yet to meet a prophet who has had a life of smooth sailing, easy success, and personal recognition. The prophetic call is a call to death. Like the apostle, the prophet must have the sentence of death in himself. He must sacrifice all for the sake of the ministry. He must die completely to self.

These are the main signs of prophetic calling. Of course, the best confirmation will always come through another prophet. God often calls a prophet to the ministry through a senior prophet. A prophet's training might come under the direction of one who has been in the prophetic office for a while.

Difference between Prophetic Ministry and the Prophetic Office

There is a difference between the prophetic ministry and the prophetic office. The first is a function, whereas the second is a position.

For I speak to you Gentiles, inasmuch as I am the apostle of the Gentiles, I magnify mine office. (Rom. 11:13)

This is a true saying, If a man desire the office of a bishop, he desireth a good work. (1 Tim. 3:1)

And let these also first be proved; then let them use the office of a deacon, being found blameless. (1 Tim. 3:10)

And verily they that are of the sons of Levi, who receive the office of the priesthood. (Heb. 7:5)

In each of these cases, you see that the term *office* is used to refer to someone who has been *permanently appointed* to a position.

This is true also of the prophetic office. The ministry of a prophet may at times be displayed by those who are not called to be prophets as permanent positions; in other words, to be in prophetic office.

Paul clarifies this when he discusses the functioning of ministries in a local church:

If any man speak in an unknown tongue, let it be by two, or at the most by three, and that by course; and let one interpret. But if there be no interpreter, let him keep silence in the church; and let him speak to himself, and to God. Let the prophets speak two or three, and let the other judge. If any thing be revealed to another that sitteth by, let the first hold his peace. For ye may all prophesy one by one, that all may learn, and all may be comforted. (1 Cor. 14:27–31)

Here Paul refers to two kinds of prophetic ministry. The first is what is communicated by the vocal gifts. Anyone who brings a message from the Lord via tongues, interpretation, or prophecy is prophesying. However, there are those who hold the office of a prophet, and they are a separate group altogether. You may all prophesy in the sense of bringing a word from the Lord, but not all the members of the church have the prophetic office.

Another passage that clearly shows the distinction is Acts 21:9–10: 'And the same man had four daughters, virgins, which did prophesy. And as we tarried [there] many days, there came down from Judaea a certain prophet, named Agabus.' Philip had four daughters who exercised a prophetic ministry, but they were not classed as prophets. Agabus, however, held the prophetic office and was referred to as a prophet.

Someone may be able to prophesy, but only when they have been permanently appointed to the prophetic office can they be called by the title of prophet. The same applies to the apostolic ministry.

Who Appoints a Prophet to Prophetic Office?

It has become the common practice among today's church organizations to ordain people to ministry. This usually involves a ceremony, but the important aspect of it is the fact that the person is given credentials by the organization to practice as a minister within that organization. A qualifying level of knowledge is usually required, and perhaps a certain amount of experience.

However, these ministry appointments are purely administrative and often have nothing to do with a person's prophetic gifts or calling. Because of this, it has become common practice to refer to those who have been ordained in this way as 'pastors'. Ordination is subject to the person continuing to hold papers with the organization.

Should that person leave the organization or fail to comply with the rules and regulations of the organization, he or she can be struck from the ordination list and have his or her credentials removed. In other words, such ordination is not a permanent possession.

These things are foreign to the prophetic ministry calling of God. The New Testament clearly teaches that the leadership ministries of the church are given and appointed by the Lord Jesus Christ, and that these gifts and callings are permanent and irrevocable.

When Moses first led the Israelites out of Egypt, he had to do all the work of counselling them and judging their disputes. When his father-in-law, Jethro, saw this, he advised Moses to appoint others to do the lower-level work, so Moses could deal personally only with difficult cases. Moses followed this advice and appointed leaders at different levels.

So Moses hearkened to the advice of his father in law, and did all that he had said. And Moses chose able men out of all Israel, and made them heads over the people, rulers of thousands, rulers of hundreds, rulers of fifties, and rulers of tens.

And they judged the people at all seasons: the difficult cases they brought to Moses, but every small matter they judged themselves. (Exod. 18:24–26)

These appointments were made by Moses, not God, and they were subject to change. They depended on Moses' decision rather than God's. Moses may have made his choices based on spiritual wisdom, but it was he and not God who appointed these rulers.

Later on, God spoke to Moses and told him to gather seventy men from among the chief leaders in Israel. God said that He would then, Himself, take the anointing that was upon Moses and place it on these seventy men also. In other words, there was going to be a spiritual transfer. These men would receive the same spiritual anointing as Moses. These were not administrative appointments. It was not Moses who was going to do this, but God Himself. And these were going to be permanent appointments.

And the Lord said unto Moses, Gather unto me seventy men of the elders of Israel, whom thou knowest to be the elders of the people, and officers over them; and bring them unto the tabernacle of the congregation, that they may stand there with thee. And I will come down and talk with thee there: and I will take of the spirit which is upon thee, and will put it upon them; and they shall bear the burden of the people with thee, that thou bear it not thyself alone. (Num. 11:16–17)

The effects of this transfer were quite clear: every person received the anointing and began to prophesy on a permanent basis. It was not a once-only anointing. This was God at work, not man.

The procedure has not changed since then. Though men and organizations might lay out their qualifications and appoint and remove people from positions of authority, it is God who calls a person to a ministry office. When God appoints people to the prophetic office, then that is what those people will be. Whether they submit to that anointing and exercise their prophetic ministry responsibility is still under their own control, because the Lord never overrides our free will. But the calling and appointment remain.

The Prophetic Office is one of the Fivefold Ministry Offices

There are five ministry offices mentioned in the New Testament. These are commonly called the fivefold ministry. However, they are far more than just ministry functions. They are all ministry offices. '(He that descended is the same also that ascended up far above all heavens, that he might fill all things.) And he gave some, apostles; and some, prophets; and some, evangelists; and some, pastors and teachers' (Eph. 4:10–11).

There are some important facts to understand about the ministry offices before you can grasp the importance of the prophetic office. To help make things clearer, we need to consider one other passage of scripture:

And God hath set some in the church, first apostles, secondarily prophets, thirdly teachers, after that miracles, then gifts of healings, helps, governments, diversities of tongues. Are all apostles? are all prophets? are all teachers? are all workers of miracles? Have all the gifts of healing? do all speak with tongues? do all interpret? (1 Cor. 12:28–30)

Here are the important facts that you need to keep in mind where ministry offices are concerned:

- The prophetic office is given by God, not man. So a person does not receive the office from human ordination, and a prophet is not subject to human authority. Prophets are subject only to the authority of the Lord.
- The prophetic office is not a local church ministry; rather, it is a gift to the body universal. In other words, when people are given a ministry office such as the office of prophet, they can exercise it anywhere in the world. It is a permanent ministry given by God.
- It is not so much that a person has been given the prophetic office, but that the office has been given in the person as a gift to the church.
- There is an order of establishment and authority among the ministries. This order is shown in the second passage above.
- Only three of the five ministries are mentioned specifically in this passage,

although the others are implied from their functions. Apostles come first. Prophets come second. Teachers come third. Evangelists and pastors come afterwards.

Paul ends his discussion in 1 Corinthians 12 by asking rhetorical questions. Are all apostles? Are all prophets? Are all teachers? And so forth. This means that not everyone can enter into a ministry office by choice. It is God who calls a person to such a ministry and imparts the office. However, these questions do not mean that a person cannot hold more than one office at a time.

There is no doubt that Paul was a teacher from the early part of his ministry. And Barnabas was clearly in prophetic office. Consider the following passage, which shows how Barnabas and Paul worked together as prophet and teacher at Antioch:

Then tidings of these things came unto the ears of the church which was in Jerusalem: and they sent forth Barnabas, that he should go as far as Antioch. Who, when he came, and had seen the grace of God, was glad, and exhorted them all, that with purpose of heart they would cleave unto the Lord. For he was a good man, and full of the

Holy Ghost and of faith: and much people was added unto the Lord. Then departed Barnabas to Tarsus, for to seek Saul: And when he had found him, he brought him unto Antioch. And it came to pass, that a whole year they assembled themselves with the church, and taught much people. And the disciples were called Christians first in Antioch. (Acts 11:22–26)

The church at Antioch started as a result of the evangelistic work of some ordinary Christians. When this happened, the apostles immediately sent them a prophet in office in the form of Barnabas, to set the church in order spiritually. In this passage we have a good description of the main function of the prophet in a local assembly. However, after a while Barnabas realized that he was lacking in the teaching ministry, and the people needed to be grounded in the Word. So he went to Tarsus to find Saul, who was clearly a teacher.

Later on, in Acts 13:1, we read of the existence at Antioch of prophets and teachers. Paul and Barnabas are listed among them. And then God instructs that Paul and Barnabas be set aside for the ministry of apostle. It is interesting that

Barnabas was more prophetic and Paul was more of a teacher. Yet together they could carry out the ministry of an apostle. This is because the apostolic function requires both of these ministries.

An apostle is able to be both a prophet and a teacher. While he was still only a teacher, Paul needed to have someone in prophetic office with him to complete the ministry. Later on, when Paul and Barnabas had a disagreement and split up, Paul found another prophet to accompany him on his journeys. Paul chose Silas as his new partner. We are told in Acts 15:32 that Silas was a prophet: 'And Judas and Silas, being prophets also themselves, exhorted the brethren with many words, and confirmed them.'

Later on in his ministry, Paul wrote to Timothy and declared that he was ordained as a preacher and an apostle and a teacher. He had entered into the fullness of his ministry and had developed into the apostolic office, which must have included prophetic ministry. 'Whereunto I am ordained a preacher, and an apostle, (I speak the truth in Christ, and lie not;) a teacher of the Gentiles in faith and verity' (1 Tim. 2:7).

Both Paul and Barnabas were called apostles. And yet they each had an additional ministry office that they did not lose. So it is possible for a person to hold more than one ministry office at the same time.

The important thing to notice here is that you do not have to remain in one ministry office. You can progress to a higher level of office. Thus the Lord can raise up an evangelist, pastor, or teacher to the prophetic office. When this happens, the prophetic office is added to the person, and the person retains the previous ministry he or she had. Such a person can now minister effectively in both areas.

If you have functioned in one of the other ministry offices, you do not need to assume that this is where your calling will remain. If you are faithful to your ministry, it is very possible that the Lord might move you to a higher position. The same thing applies to both ministry offices and gifts of the Spirit. Paul encourages us to earnestly desire the better gifts and to follow after love. As you do this, the way is open for the Lord to lead you further.

The Different Types of Prophet

- Prophets to the nation (Amos 3:7)
- Teaching prophets (Acts 13:1)
- Prophets that pronounce God's judgment (Jer. 1:16–17) and execute God's judgment (Rev.11:3–13)
- Seers (1 Sam. 9:9)
- Weeping prophets or intercessors Lamentation
- Writing prophets (Ezra)
- Prophets to the local assembly of the body of Christ (1 Cor. 12:28)
- Travelling prophets/missionaries Acts

Evangelist

The gift of evangelism is the particular ability that Christ gives to some members of His church to share the good news with unbelievers in such a way that sinners become the disciples of Jesus and responsible members of the body of Christ.

An evangelist has a special ability to gather people together and unique anointing to make known the gospel of our Lord Jesus Christ, such that many people respond. Evangelists are actively passionate about the soul of the sinner; they are interested in the salvation of the unsaved.

Although all Christians are called to witness Christ to sinners and win souls to God's kingdom, this does not mean that all Christians occupy the office of evangelist.

Evangelism is the act of presenting the gospel to unbelievers in the power of the Holy Spirit, with a view to bringing them to accept Jesus Christ as Lord and Saviour and to nurture them until Christ is truly formed in them so that they bear fruit for Christ.

Evangelism is never good news about a particular church, denomination, or pastor. It is not an argument about a religion. It is not a title for decoration. It is not an argument about differences in religious practice. It is not an argument and or explanation about a religious belief.

Evangelists are called and anointed by God. They are the bells of the church. They have passion and vision for the unsaved. They are very dynamic in outreaches, crusades, or other platforms given to win souls for Christ. They find fulfilment whenever they have opportunity to gather others into God's kingdom.

Genuine evangelists are willing to be spent and unspent to win a soul to God's kingdom. They rarely conclude a service without an altar call. Their heartbeats are soul winning, and they mostly have the gifts of healing, miracles, faith, wisdom, help, and revelation.

Evangelists should not turn themselves into administrators, pastors, or deliverance ministers.

The office of an evangelist is not just a title. It is a calling to gather sinners to repentance unto Christ. It is not an office to be used to raise funds. You must not lose focus.

Pastor

In the New Testament, the terms *elder, presbyter, overseer bishop,* and *pastor* are used interchangeably to denote those charged with the leadership of the gathering of God's people. However, there is a difference between the *office* of pastor and the *gift* of pastor.

Many people called to ministry today answer to the title of pastor, but this is not scriptural. That you graduate from a seminary, theology school, or Bible school does not make you a pastor. The school simply trains and thoroughly equips you for kingdom service. Callings are not distributed in schools. *No!*

An evangelist who has gone to a Bible school for one to three years is still an evangelist. Some people graduate first as evangelists and are eventually ordained as pastors when promoted. This also is not scriptural. The office of pastor is not greater than that of evangelist; neither is it less than that of an apostle. Each of the ministerial offices and callings is unique and differs only in responsibilities. The office of an apostle may have higher responsibilities than that of a pastor; that does not make one office greater than the other.

The gift of a pastor, according to Dr C. Peter Wagner, is 'the special ability that God gives to certain members of the body of Christ to assume a long-term personal responsibility for the spiritual welfare of a group of believers.'

A pastor is one who is given the responsibility of nurturing the church, or body of Christ, with the Word of God. A pastor cares for the wellbeing of the congregants and sees to their welfare, not only spiritually but in other areas – physical, material, and so on.

Hence, pastors are rightly expected to divide the Word of truth to feed the flock of God. But they are not only to feed the flock. They are also to watch over them jealously, prayerfully showing concern for their well-being.

Pastors have a heart for their flocks. They see their flocks' problems as their own and their flocks' needs as their own. They watch over their flocks with care and ensure their flocks do not derail from the will of God. They guide them with God's Word; they rebuke, correct, teach, and preach sound doctrine to help Christ's flock to flourish. They are always on the watch in prayers, not only for their family members but for the whole flock of God.

Genuine pastors can spend and be spent for Christ's flock. Their desire is to see the flock grow and flourish in God's will and counsel. They are never tired meeting the flock's needs.

Gifted pastors have thick shock absorbers to accommodate people's problems and to lead them before God for solutions. Good preaching and teaching abilities are other signs of the pastoral gift, but not all preachers or teachers are gifted pastors.

Most pastors help to pasture their flocks with the Word of God. Pastors pour out their spirituals treasures and attention on others; they give people their patience and personal interaction over a long period. Pastors often have, among other gifts, the gifts of administration, exhortation, mercy, help, wisdom, discernment, and teaching.

Teacher

Teachers are those who are called and anointed by God to effectively communicate the divine counsel of God, as stated in the Word of God, in such a way that everyone can live practically with it, without being confused. Teachers have the special ability to disseminate God's written counsel to all, such that the weak and the strong can effectively understand the mind of God.

Teachers are Bible exponents who are not allegorical but factual communicators of divine messages. They are spiritual researchers who have inner ears to hear and understanding hearts to grasp the meaning of biblical codes and symbols.

Teachers are speakers who always have relevant illustrations to impress divine messages into the heart of believers. Their divine gift usually leaves no doubt in the mind of the audience as to what God intends. Such teachers are different from ordinary, secular, professional teachers who may find themselves in the church. Although all pastors are expected to be apt at teaching, not all pastors are good teachers. That a man attends a teacher training college does not qualify him to be a teacher in the body of Christ. A professor of education may not be able to teach the Word of God with divine accuracy and explanation.

If God has called you to be a teacher, do not take the role of an administrator or an evangelist. Develop yourself and exercise your teaching gift.

Teachers are often noted to be lovers of books. They love to seek knowledge. They are good readers and speakers. They carry a special grace to interpret and explain the scriptures with profound insight, making difficult puzzles simple. They are fearless when expounding God's Word.

Most often they have the gifts of words, knowledge, wisdom, discernment, and other vocal gifts.

Motivator (or Creator)

Apostles, prophets, evangelists, pastors, and teachers are often regarded as recipients of the ministerial gift, sometimes referred to as the pulpit ministry. Those called into any of these offices are regarded as the pulpit ministers. They can be full-time or part-time ministers. The most important thing is that they are called by God and anointed by God to serve in these offices.

Although today we have people who are called into the pulpit ministry by God, we have some who are called into the ministry by men and others who go into the ministry of their own accord. Some people are led to start a ministry out of frustration, some because they do not know what else to do, and some out of hunger. Very few are divinely called.

Whichever category you fall into, there is no doubt that, when the time comes, your work will be tested by fire. If it be of God, it will stand; if not, it will be consumed.

Besides the pulpit ministry, there are the motivation or creational gifts of God the Father. 'Now there are diversities of gifts, but the same Spirit. And there are differences of administrations, but the same Lord. And there are diversities of operations, but it is the same God which worketh all in all' (1 Cor. 12:4–6). A role in ministry is not restricted to the pulpit ministry alone. There are roles in the ministry that God has called men to work.

Servant

The gift of service is a motivational gift of God the Father. This gift is a special ability given to certain members of the body of Christ to identify unmet needs relating to God's work, and then to meet these needs by making use of available resources.

Those endowed with this gift are willing to be spent totally for God's work. They not only release their finances, they also release their energy. They are people best regarded as those who love the Lord their God with all their might, minds, and hearts.

Those whose calling includes 'public ministry' or 'official duty' are public servants (2 Cor. 9:12; Phil. 2:17, 30; Heb. 8:6; Rom. 13:6). Examples include highly positioned and influential people in society who partake in the building project of a church, like carrying blocks, planks, concrete, and other building materials. They are physically and personally involved in such projects. They are exceptionally humble, quite unassuming, and display tolerance and forbearance.

People with this gift need not be forced to do such works in the house of God; they are naturally willing to do these tasks and do not need commendation from men.

Exorcist (or Deliverer)

The gift of exorcism is the ability God has given to some members of the body of Christ to cast out demons from people and other creations of God.

All spirit-filled Christians, to a reasonable extent, ought to be able to discern the presence of an evil spirit in the activities of people under satanic possession, but those with the gift of exorcism have an extraordinary grace to discern the names, titles, and works of demons in their victims.

There are diverse opinions about the deliverance ministry. In some places it is considered the same thing as the healing ministry. But there is a difference between healing and delivering.

Not everyone has the special gift of deliverance. The Bible, from the Old Testament to the New Testament, gives various records of God commanding deliverance for His people. For example, there is the deliverance of His people from the hand of Pharaoh in Exodus 12:51: 'And it came to pass the selfsame day, *[that]* the LORD did bring the children of Israel out of the land of Egypt by their armies.'

In the New Testament, the Lord appointed the twelve disciples and sent them:

Behold, I give unto you power to tread on serpents and scorpions, and over all the power of the enemy: and nothing shall by any means hurt you. (Luke 10:19)

And he said unto them, Go ye into all the world, and preach the gospel to every creature. He that believeth and is baptized shall be saved; but he that believeth not shall be damned. ... it shall not hurt them; they shall lay hands on the sick, and they shall recover. (Mark 16:15–18)

Many times when people are evangelized and invited to church, they come with their problems and challenges. Most times they are possessed, obsessed, or oppressed by demons. The fact remains that, as long as they are not fully delivered, they are a trouble to the church.

Knowledge of God's Word can set these people free. There are certain believers in the body of

Christ who have been called, gifted, and anointed to minister such deliverance.

It was said of Jesus, 'God anointed Jesus of Nazareth with the Holy Ghost and with power: who went about doing good, and healing all that were oppressed of the devil; for God was with him' (Acts 10:38). Most times, those who are gifted with exorcism have the gifts of miracles, healings, and sometimes prophetic unction. They may be gifted also in intercession, fasting to receive keys, and taking extra caution not to become victims of bounce-back attacks.

Exhorter

Many people in the body of Christ today suffer unnecessarily from ignorance as well as unfavourable circumstances and situations. They are troubled and broken-hearted. They need encouragement or counsel to ease their burdened souls.

Some believers have been given special abilities and anointing to lift these burdens from the others' minds. They are called *counsellors* or exhorters.

Most Christians have taken after wrong counsels received from ungodly friends or even Christian brethren who were not genuine exhorters. Some have made decisions that ruined their lives as a result.

Although all pastors and shepherds are expected to have the gift of counsel, not all shepherds are exhorters. We need genuine exhorters today. Through the work of genuine exhorters, many who have troubled destinies could get relief, and many who are disturbed, perplexed, or cheated in their lives could receive comfort.

One of the greatest challenges for Christians today is how to get connected to genuinely anointed exhorters who are specifically gifted to help them when they are in trouble. Deprived world systems, with their polluting standards and unpalatable conditions, often compel us to face hard realities. New believers in particular have had their lives subjected to the rule of Satan before they meet Christ. Some are hard drug addicts, some prostitutes. Others are broken hearted, rejected, cheated, oppressed, or barren. And they believe that the church is God's embassy on earth. True exhorters are divinely empowered to attend to each category of new converts, after which these young believers feel encouraged, helped, and healed so that they wish to remain in the church.

The aggressive and effective evangelistic outreaches of the church of Jesus Christ, without an anointed follow-up exhorter's team to help and encourage the young converts, will be like a mighty wave of noise that shall soon evaporate into the air. Counsellors should be trained to handle each of the human groups or problems in the church.

Every pastor should aspire to be a counsellor, one who is willing to listen to others, partake of their problems, discern what to do, proffer solutions, do them, and keep issues confidential.

Every counsellor should know where to refer difficult cases.

Exhorters should be people given to prayer and the Word. They must not see themselves as all-wise people who do not need to be counselled too. We must remember that the Holy Spirit is the greatest comforter and counsellor, and that in the multitude of counsel, there is safety.

Generous Giver

This is the special ability given to some people in the body of Christ to give beyond the natural ability to meet the needs of men and women and to advance the work of God on earth.

Those who have this gift are always willing to sacrifice all they have to assist or advance God's work. They first give of themselves and then of their substance absolutely for God. They can give anything in their possession to help others or advance God's work. They are like God's bankers on earth, cashing the cheques God issues to finance His work on earth.

Generous givers are known to be persistent seed sowers. They are the best financial secretaries and treasurers; they are often sympathetic and empathetic. They do not need to be persuaded to give – they are willing to give, and find a sense of fulfilment when they empty themselves for others or for the advancement of God's work. For them lack is far away; they carry the blessings of God upon them. They are mostly positive thinkers.

Hospitable One

'Use hospitality one to another without grudging. As every man hath received the gift, *[even so]* minister the same one to another, as good stewards of the manifold grace of God' (1 Pet. 4:9–10). The gift of hospitality is the special ability given to certain people in the body of Christ to accommodate and take care of people, even when the people are unknown to them.

People with the gift of hospitality can accommodate strangers in their own houses and feed them without complaint. They are happy when people come to stay with them. They are always glad; they provide their lodgers with everything they can afford to make their stay comfortable. Some hospitable ones have, in such a way, entertained angels.

Missionary

But the Lord said unto him, Go your way: for he is a chosen vessel unto me, to bear my name before the Gentiles, and kings, and the children of Israel. (Acts 9:15)

Whereof I was made a minister, according to the gift of the grace of God given unto me by the effective working of his power. (Eph. 3:7)

The gift of the missionary is the special ability given to some people in the body of Christ to preach the gospel and make disciples of people, often outside their own cultures and languages. Being a missionary often requires leaving one's comfort base to go to another place, ethnic group, or tribe to preach and make disciples for Christ.

Most often, missionaries are sent. They are usually apostles. They break new ground, start new works, plant new churches, and establish new converts. They may be persecuted for their faith. They bring the gospel where it has not been heard before, and after the gospel has been established in one place, they go to another. They can spend several years in a place, learning the inhabitants' culture, language, and ways so as to penetrate them with the gospel.

Merciful One

Mercy is showing compassionate love and kindness without expecting anything in return. The gift of mercy extends to people outside the fold of Christ. It reaches to all.

People with this gift are often seen visiting motherless babies, leper colonies, centres for the blind, and other such places to make their contribution.

Merciful ones are different from those who visit the needy with a cameraman or videographer with the aim of announcing their generosity. Such attention-seekers get their reward from the applause and commendations of men, or from funds extorted from the public for their personal interest.

Those with the gift of mercy donate medical supplies, food, and other materials without any unnecessary noise.

Helper

Unlike the gift of mercy, the gift of help is directed to one person at a time. Mercy includes both Christians and non-Christians, while those with the gift of help focus on other Christians. They are like Aaron and Joshua, who held the hands of Moses.

Those with the gift of help are like burden sharers who make the burden of a particular person of God lighter. Some help in voluntary services, others in transcribing and writing books, and so forth. Some helpers volunteer to intercede for the person of God, or give a certain amount to a ministry regularly. They make the work easier for the pulpit ministers in many ways, although help ministry is not restricted to the pulpit ministers alone.

Celibate

But he said unto them, All men cannot receive this saying, save they to whom it is given. For there are some eunuchs, which were so born from their mother's womb: and there are some eunuchs, which were made eunuchs of men: and there be eunuchs, which have made themselves eunuchs for the kingdom of heaven's sake. He that is able to receive it, let him receive it. (Matt. 19:11–12)

For I would that all men were even as myself. But every man hath his proper gift of God, one after this manner, and another after that. (1 Cor. 7:7)

The gift of celibacy is a special gift given to some people in the body of Christ, who deny themselves marriage because of their work in the kingdom of God.

Not all people have this special grace; those with the gift are relatively few. Those who have this gift do not have any sexual drive. If there is such a drive in you consistently, it means you don't have the gift.

God has not forbidden you from marriage, and marriage does not disqualify you from serving God. It rather enables you to serve God all the more. Living in pretence only makes you waste your life. If you are not called into celibacy, do not pretend you are. You will serve God better if you are married than if you pretend to be a celibate.

Leader

This is a special ability that God has given to certain members of the church to initiate goals and objectives in accordance with God's mind and purpose. Leaders influence their church communities to pursue God's purpose in such a way that the people willingly and harmoniously work together. Leaders are generally regarded as people of influence – people with the ability to motivate others to respond to God's set objective.

As sound as leadership training can be outside the church, secular training is nothing when compares to the kingdom principles of leadership. The error Christians make today is to take lesson from business schools and establish business principles as rules for the church to obey.

God's kingdom cannot be governed by carnal minds. God has His provision for His church. What He does not provide for, He does not need. The Bible is full of lessons illustrating the mind of God with regard to leadership. We do not need master's degrees in business administration to effectively act as church leaders.

This does not mean that education is useless. God can use it, but it is not the basis for a leadership position. God's Word and principles are the basis. Effective leadership in God's kingdom means leading God's people by God's principles as stated in the scriptures.

Administrator

Not every leader is an administrator, but every administrator is a leader. An administrator plans, organizes, controls, coordinates, represents, decides, delegates, evaluates, creates, and leads.

The gift of administration is the divine grace that God gives to some Christians to understand with clarity the immediate and long-term goals of the church. Administrators devise and execute success strategies to attain these goals.

Martyr

Martyrs are those who bear witness by their deaths. The gift of martyrdom is the special empowerment of God in some Christians, such that they undergo severe suffering and affliction for their faith, even to the point of death, while consistently displaying a positive, joyous, and victorious attitude that glorifies God.

When they heard these things, they were cut to the heart, and they gnashed on him with their teeth. But he, being full of the Holy Ghost, looked up stedfastly into heaven, and saw the glory of God, and Jesus standing on the right hand of God, And said, Behold, I see the heavens opened, and the Son of man standing on the right hand of God. Then they cried out with a loud voice, and stopped their ears, and ran upon him with one accord, And cast him out of the city, and stoned him: and the witnesses laid down their clothes at a young man's feet, whose name was Saul. And they stoned Stephen, calling upon God, and saying, Lord Jesus, receive my spirit. And he kneeled down, and cried with a loud voice, Lord, lay not this sin to their charge. And when he had said this, he fell asleep. (Acts 7:54–60)

Volunteer for Poverty

The gift of voluntary poverty is a special ability given to certain members of the body of Christ to willingly deny themselves comfort and pleasure for the sake of the kingdom of God. These people may have opportunities to enrich themselves or live comfortable lives, but would rather divert their riches to other services of God.

People with this gift are relatively few, but it was recorded that the late Apostle Ayo Babalola had this gift. The living legend Professor Zaccanah Tannee formum (Cameroon) is considered to have had this gift.

In conclusion, everyone who is born again has at least one spiritual gift from God. Those who are not born again, however, do not have a gift.

Every human being has a talent. A talent is different from a spiritual gift. Your talent is given to you for profit. You can turn your talents into money.

After new birth, God may make your talents into your spiritual gift. For example, Peter was a fisherman who became a fisher of men. Some people are naturally good at talking or making speeches before their new births; after their new births, they may be gifted exhorters.

No matter what your area of calling, you should properly use your gift as a Christian to serve God.

To discover and maximize your gift as a Christian:

- You must be born again.
- You must believe that you are endowed with a spiritual gift.
- You must be ready to work and make a profit with the gift.
- You must pray for God's guidance.
- You must explore – study, read, search, and seek to know more about all spiritual

gifts. Move closer to mentors and people with higher knowledge who know better and have the gift. Ask them questions.

- You must practice your gifts as much as possible.

- You must examine peace of mind and joy.

- You must evaluate: Are you producing results? Are God's people edified and blessed after you exercise your gift?

- You must expect a confirmation from the body of Christ.

- You must seek education. Knowledge is better than strength. Seek to know and be better trained.

- You must exercise. Use your gift daily to make it stronger.

7.
ROLES IN GOVERNANCE

Roles in governance differ. They include all manner of jobs and careers – bricklaying, tailoring, teaching, trading, and politics. However, we can, for simplicity's sake, divide the roles in governance into three areas: roles in politics, roles in business, and roles in government.

God is not a God of mistakes. From the creation of the harmful scorpion to the creation of the nutritious rabbit in the field, God has a specific purpose for each thing that exists. Everybody may not have roles to play in the pulpit, but God has called each and every one of us into certain and specific assignments in life. It is the discovery of these assignments that is called *purpose*, and the attainment of purpose brings fulfilment. When one's assignment is left undiscovered, a portion of the earth is left unstable. The consequence is that generations suffer unless there is a fast replacement.

The omissions of past heroes comprise the mission fighting against us today. If we fail to identify and fulfil our roles today, generations after us will have more potholes to fill. Yesterday is for your ancestors, today is yours, and tomorrow is for your children.

The problems of today are an accumulation of the omissions of yesterday. And the trouble of tomorrow, if it exists, will be the accumulation of the omissions of yesterday and today. Generations to come will not forgive us if we ignore our responsibility to secure a better tomorrow for our children. It was Benjamin Franklin who said, 'Plough deep while sluggards sleep, and you shall have corn to sell and keep.' He also said, 'Work as if you were to live one hundred years, pray as if you were to die tomorrow.'

Roles in Politics

It is not a lie that God calls His people into politics to establish His kingdom. It is, however, disheartening that men who have taken politics as a platform to fulfil His counsel have done so to build monuments for themselves. Politics is a divine arrangement by which godly leaders can minister God's counsel to the people. It is a platform allowed by God to enable reasonable coordination and dissemination of God's counsel among men. Joseph was a politician. Daniel was a politician. And they fulfilled God's counsel.

We have been called upon by God to pray for those in government, for they are God's agents to execute justice upon those who are disobedient. But those who are to execute justice are the ones violating the rules. One unique truth about men and women in the Bible who fulfilled God's counsel from the platform of politics is that they all understood the purpose for which God sent them. Joseph knew he was to preserve the seed of Jacob during the famine. Esther understood she was to rescue Israel from destruction. Daniel was aware he was to establish God's kingdom rulership. They all understood the purpose for which the Lord called them into politics, and they fulfilled it. They did not just sit and imagine what the need of the masses was so as to attend to it. As good as that may seem, it is not God's way of leadership.

For it to be God's, it must start with God. If what you call a vision is a mere expression of sympathy for the masses, you have done well but have not satisfied God's counsel and purpose.

Most people in politics have high callings. They are like apostles in the political world. But rather than pursue the assignment God has given them in God's way, they choose a carnal, unfruitful method and get unfruitful result. It would be very pleasant if politicians could find time to be alone with God, to learn from Him His ways of doing things, rather than pursuing winds.

The unfortunate story these ungodly politicians have yet to be told is that the consequences of negligence are greater than the pleasures they are enjoying now. Truly, God needs men and women in politics, but as He did with David, God will train and test them – then trust them. Politicians are first required to understand God's purpose for sending them into politics and God's principles for effective leadership.

The study of the lives and stories of David, Nehemiah, Joseph, Daniel, Esther, and even Saul are good lesson material for politicians. After all, their lives are examples for us, that we may glean truth from their strengths and weaknesses.

To be effective in an assignment as a politician, you must understand that political offices are simply God-given platforms for the purpose of fulfilling God's counsel. A politician or aspiring politician should first of all seek to understand what God's purpose is – what assignment He wants you to do. You must constantly remind yourself of the day of reckoning. This is vital.

Choose godly relationships that can help you in actualising God's purposes. Wrong company ruined Saul, though he was the first anointed king of Israel. Right strategy or methods, divinely inspired, are tools for effective leadership in politics.

Roles in Business

Servant, obey in all things your masters according to the flesh; not with eyeservice as menpleasers, but in singleness of heart, fearing God: And whatsoever ye do, do it heartily as to the Lord, and not unto men. Knowing that of the Lord ye shall receive the reward of the inheritance: for ye serve the Lord Christ. But he that doeth wrong shall receive for the wrong which he hath done: and there is no respect of persons. (Col. 3:22–25)

Masters, give unto your servants that which is just and equal: knowing that ye also have a Master in heaven. (Col. 4:1)

Whether you are working under somebody or you are the owner of a business, God has a role for you to play. You need to master your role to play it effectively. Some individuals have been empowered by God to solve the problem of unemployment in their generation. Such people may make more money by accident than on purpose, according to God's intent to help them fulfil their purpose on earth. While God may call on some to solve the problem of unemployment, He may also choose to disciple an employee under an employer for a leadership role in the future.

In whatever capacity you find yourself, either as the boss or the servant, seek to understand what impact and contribution God has empowered you to make via your platform to your generation.

Do not forget that unfaithfulness in doing God's will for your life will cause a setback in your journey, your reward, and the lives of generations after you, including your children. 'If therefore ye have not been faithful in the unrighteous mammon, who will commit to your trust the true *[riches]*? And if ye have not been faithful in that which is another man's, who shall give you that which is your own?' (Luke 16:11–12).

Even in a one-man business, ensure just weights and measures, and be honest and fair to your customers. This is God's principle in business. Seek to understand God's purpose for your business. There is nothing you own on earth today that is not given to you by the Lord. You are a mere steward of God's resources. They are under your trust, and you will surely give account on the last day.

So seek to understand why God has so blessed you and given you a business or made you work for a particular establishment. Pursue that purpose. You will then see and take the flight of God.

Roles in Government

It's rather unfortunate that most civil servants in developing countries go to work only for the fun of it, simply to earn a living. Some do not report to work at all; some do so at will. They come to work at the time of their choice and leave work at their desired time. They believe that, since it is not their work, little attention is needed or required of them.

That is a major reason why most civil servants cannot have their own businesses after retirement; if they do, those businesses do not last long, because they developed very bad habits. When they do try, they end up as failures.

Human beings tend to forget that God is just and a rewarder. You cannot be nonchalant as a public servant and expect your private business to thrive. God is just; what you sow, you will surely reap. That is one of the slogans of life itself.

God's principles are eternal; they don't change. If you are unfaithful in that which is another man's, nobody will commit unto your trust your own.

The word of the Lord is clear: 'And whatsoever ye do, do it heartily, as to the Lord, and not unto men!' (Col. 3:23). This is a valid truth: we must approach every service as unto the Lord and not unto men.

We are in public service for a purpose. Seek God in prayer and ask Him to reveal to you why He has chosen you for the place you occupy. God is willing to talk to you as a son or a daughter if you are willing to hear. God's Word is light to guide you into His will for your life.

Let your service to others be unto the Lord and not unto men. Serve in honesty and with humility, that the lives of others be touched by the love of Christ through your service. Through your service, men and women may see the love of Christ and come to God.

There may be several reasons why God has called you to public service:

- You will help God's will and counsel be established. So seek to know God's will.
- You will help to make Christ known to those who do not know Him. You will do this through your service in the love of Christ, a public service. May God grant you understanding. The general will of God prevails in any service, whether political or private.
- The needs of others will be met in the love of Christ through your service.
- You may provide for your own household and live in comfort.

8.
ROLES IN FAMILY

And the Lord said, shall I hide from Abraham that thing which I do; Seeing that Abraham shall surely become a great and mighty nation, and all the nations of the earth shall be blessed in him? For I know him, that he will command his children and his household after him, and they shall keep the way of the Lord, to do justice and judgment; that the Lord may bring upon Abraham that which he hath spoken of him. (Gen. 18:17–19)

God has a very special plan for the family. It is the first institution God initiated. The troubles in society today are a result of omission in the family. If every family existed in accordance with the pattern of God's will, many troubles and problems in our society today would not exist.

The family is regarded as the smallest unit of society. All parents are expected to train their children in the way of the Lord. 'Train up a child in the way he should go: and when he is old, he will not depart from it' (Prov. 22:6). If all parents played their roles effectively – bringing up their children in the way of the Lord, teaching them the Word of God on a daily basis, and finding time to pray for and with them – things would change greatly.

Loving your child does not mean excluding discipline. Spank them when they misbehave; as the saying goes, 'Spare the rod and spoil the child.' You can instil discipline in their lives by beating them when necessary. 'He that spareth his rod hateth his son: but he that loveth him chasteneth him betimes' (Prov. 13:24). There is no civilization that nullifies God's Word if God approves the use of the rod to discipline a child. Civilization should not modernize God's Word. If your children need a rebuke, rebuke them, or you will destroy their future. Do not over-pamper them. You will make them cheap for the future.

Teach your children the needful domestic works they are expected to know. Be sure to guide them in the way of the Lord. What you refuse to teach your children at home, they will be taught outside. This may become a source of trouble in their lives.

Chasten thy son while there is hope, and let not thy soul spare for his crying. (Prov. 19:18)

Foolishness *[is]* bound in the heart of a child; *[but]* the rod of correction shall drive it far from him. (Prov. 22:15)

The rod and reproof give wisdom: but a child left *[to himself]* bringeth his mother to shame. (Prov. 29:15)

Correct thy son, and he shall give thee rest; yea, he shall give delight unto thy soul. (Prov. 29:17)

Questions

- In one sentence, describe who you are and what you are meant to be.
- If you had all you ever desired financially, list ten things you would do.
- Mention four key people in your life with whom you would never desire to lose contact. State why.
- Mention four key people you would like to pattern your life after. State why.

- What factors did you consider before writing your answer to question one?
- What problem did you solve recently or what need did you meet that made you happy?
- What do you need to do more so as to be a better person to yourself, your neighbour, your community, and your nation?

PART III

At the end of this section, you will have an understanding of the following:

- God's provisions for your divinely assigned roles
- Keys to functioning in your divinely assigned roles
- The cost of fulfilling divinely assigned roles

In life, God has made provision for every vision.
Every vision suffering a setback is either not from
God or the provision has not been sought for.
—OluwaFemi Lanre-Oke

No one is either rich or poor who has not helped
himself to be so.
—German Proverb

Life is not holding a good hand; life is playing a
poor hand well.
—Danish proverb

9.
GOD'S PROVISIONS FOR YOUR DIVINELY ASSIGNED ROLES

Provisions are what God makes available to you to help you achieve or accomplish a vision, assignment, or role. For us to play our roles effectively, God makes available provisions to make the pursuit and fulfilment of our roles easier. Some of these provisions are:

- Anointing/callings
- Money
- Possessions
- Positions
- Skills
- Energy
- People

Anointing/Callings

For the purpose of this book, I shall restrict the discussion of anointing and calling to the pulpit ministries. Pulpit ministers are the coaches of all other destinies; they equip others to fulfil their roles in life. God gives the anointing and callings upon individuals to play certain critical roles: 'For the perfecting of the saints, for the work of the ministry, for the edifying of the body of Christ' (Eph. 4:12). The anointing upon such people empowers them to function in the supernatural and hence enables them to fulfil their roles effectively.

People in this category have callings as apostles, prophets, pastors, teachers, evangelists, or a combination of two or more of these positions. Pulpit ministers understand that these offices are not opportunities to exploit others or to lord it over them, but rather means of fulfilling the mandate and counsel of God.

Money

Certain people, because of the nature of the roles they are meant to play in life, will have the privilege of access to larger amounts of money than others. Their roles require more money, so God gives them grace and strength for financial prosperity so they can fulfil such roles.

A problem arises when the person concerned is ignorant of the reason that God gave him or her such opportunity for financial increase. Rather than use the blessing for its purpose, the person might squander the money on frivolous things.

The Bible speaks about people who ministered unto Jesus out of their substance. This is an example of using resources according to purpose.

And it came to pass afterward, that he went throughout every city and village, preaching and showing the glad tidings of the kingdom of God: and the twelve were with him, And certain women, who had been healed of evil spirits and infirmities, Mary called Magdalene, out of whom went seven demons, And Joanna the wife of Chuza Herod's steward, and Susanna, and many others, who ministered unto him of their substance. (Luke 8:1–3)

Possessions

There are certain people who are given possessions to help them effectively play their roles in life. These people may not be extremely wealthy in terms of money, but they have either inherited or been given material things of value. Some people may not need to buy clothes or shoes. This does not mean they cannot afford to buy; it is simply unnecessary for them to do so. They have a lot of such material possessions – to such an extent that, if well channelled to the purpose God intended, it would be a huge blessing to the benefactor.

A key example of a person who used her material possessions rightly is the woman with the alabaster box:

Now when Jesus was in Bethany, in the house of Simon the leper, There came unto him a woman having an alabaster box of very precious ointment, and poured it on his head, as he sat at meat. But when his disciples saw it, they had indignation, saying, To what purpose is this waste? For this ointment might have been sold for much, and given to the poor. When Jesus understood it, he said unto them, Why trouble ye the woman? for she hath wrought a good work upon me. For ye have the poor always with you; but me ye have not always. For in that she hath poured this ointment on my body, she did it for my burial. Verily I say unto you, Whersoever this gospel shall be preached in the whole world, there shall also this, that this woman hath done, be told for a memorial of her. (Matt. 26:6–13)

This woman had a precious ointment in her possession. She understood for what purpose it had been given her, and she used it for the purpose at the right time. Other women in Mark 16:1 had also wanted to fulfil this role, but in their case it was too late. When they got there with their oil, the Lord was no longer there. They had the oil, but their timing was wrong for using it.

And when the sabbath was past, Mary Magdalene, and Mary the mother of James, and Salome, had bought sweet spices, that they might come and anoint him. (Mark 16:1)

And he saith unto them, Be not affrighted: Ye seek Jesus of Nazareth, which was crucified: he is risen; he is not here: behold the place where they laid him. (Mark 16:6)

God gives you possessions to enable you play your role well. Are you using those possessions to glorify God, or are you using them to cause others to stumble?

Positions

For us to fulfil our divinely assigned roles, God gives us positions. But positions differ from one person to another, depending on what role God has chosen them to play. Esther, for example, needed to occupy the position of queen so as to fulfil her God-given role. She was chosen by God to rescue the children of Israel from destruction, but that role could not be fulfilled if there were no highly exalted position for her. Queen Vasht needed to misbehave and be removed in order for God's candidate to be selected.

It would have been rather unfortunate if Esther had forgotten the purpose for which God gave her the position she was occupying. As we learn in Esther 4:14, the position was not the reason that God called her. The assignment to rescue the

Israelites was her purpose. For the purpose to be fulfilled, that position was needed. And for her to qualify for the position, beauty was needed. So God gave her beauty to qualify her for the position that would enable her to fulfil her assignment in life.

You must understand that each of your gifts from God is given to enable you to fulfil the purpose of God for your life. 'And who knoweth when thou art come to the kingdom for such a time as this' (Esther 4:14).

In Esther 4:1–17, we learn that Mordecai was another person to whom God gave a position. He was the queen's uncle, yet he was the man at the gate. Mordecai had to play the role of mentor to Esther in order for God's counsel to be fulfilled. God uniquely chose Mordecai to play the role, and he played it effectively. He engineered the queen into taking godly steps that would actualize God's counsel for God's people.

Joseph is another example of a man who was given a position to fulfil God's counsel. Israel needed to be preserved from the famine to come, and Joseph was instrumental in achieving that preservation. God eventually arranged for Joseph to fulfil his purpose by righting every wrong intention of the people who surrounded him.

God has a way of making everything work together for our good so that His counsel for our lives can be fulfilled. You are not a creature of error; you are what you are because of the reason behind your existence. You might not be occupying a key position like Joseph or Esther, but God can make you a Mordecai. Though only a gatekeeper, Mordecai was highly relevant to God's counsel.

Do not envy those who occupy high positions. God has placed them there so that they might fulfil His counsel. Promotion does not come from the West or from the East but from the Lord. As prominent as the face of a person is, it cannot ignore the small intestine. If the small intestine decides to be seen as the face is seen, then death is certain. Your own position may be as a classroom teacher, military officer, doctor, nurse, lawyer, engineer, department head, manager, assistant, or common officer. Whatever it is, discover why God has placed you there, and fulfil your role effectively.

Skills

There are people who understand how to do certain things exceptionally well. We must not forget that we all have this sort of provision from God for the purposes of glorifying God and meeting the needs of others – in other words, to solve problems. Whatsoever God gives you is not to help create another problem but to solve one.

An example of someone who used her skill in fulfilling God's counsel was Dorcas. She made coats and gave them to others. Her actions contributed to her longevity.

Now there was at Joppa a certain disciple named Tabitha, which by interpretation is called Dorcas: this woman was full of good works and almsdeeds which she did. And it came to pass in those days, that she was sick, and died: whom when they had washed, they laid her in an upper chamber. And forasmuch as Lydia was nigh to Joppa, and the disciples had heard that peter was there, they sent unto him two men, desiring him that he would not delay to come to them. Then peter arose and went with them. When he was come, they brought him into the upper chamber: and all the widows stood by him weeping, and shewing the coats and garments which Dorcas made, while she was with them. But Peter put them all forth, and kneeled down, and prayed; and turning him to the body said, Tabitha arise. And she opened her eyes: and when she saw Peter, she sat up. (Acts 9:36–40)

Energy

Energy is part of what God gives people so they can play their roles effectively in life. Energy is commonly defined as the capacity or ability to perform work. We all have energy but to different extents, depending on the roles we are to play.

We cannot compare the bones in the ear with the bones of the hand. They are different because of the different purposes they serve. Certain people are given more energy than others to work or do service in the household of God, because their roles differ.

A key example of a man with this kind of provision is Simon, a Cyrenian: 'And as they led him away, they laid hold upon one Simon, a Cyrenian coming out of the country, and on him they laid the cross, that he might bear it after Jesus' (Luke 23:26).

The only reason you are alive is your purpose. You must discover it and fulfil it. Understand what God has made available for you and what God has given you to fulfil it. You must not forget that everything God has brought you – friends, gifts, people, revelation – is for a single purpose: that you might discover who you are in Him and fulfil the purpose for which He has created you.

Nobody would have heard about Simon but for the cross of Jesus. Carrying the cross was what he was created to do. If he had failed to do it, God would have raised an alternative in his stead, and Simon would not have been part of God's movement on earth. You read about Simon now because he discovered his assignment – his provision – and he used it effectively.

People

In truth, nobody can fulfil a destiny in isolation. God did not. He said, 'Let us make man in our image' (Gen. 1:26). God made consultations. Jesus Christ, our leader, did not. He waited to choose twelve disciples who would be with Him and whom He might send forth to preach (Mark 3:14).

We all need others so that we may fulfil our roles in life. The head cannot say to the leg, 'I do not need you.' They both need each other. But God gives to certain people a unique collection of contacts for the sake of the assignment or role they are to fulfil.

Such people may or may not be financially wealthy, but they are connected. They can link you up to the governor of your state or the president of the nation. Securing a job opportunity is not a problem; they know a person who knows another person who owns a company.

An example of such a man is Joseph the Arimathea. In Mark 15:43–45, we learn that, after the death of Jesus Christ, our Lord and Saviour, on the cross of Calvary, there was need to bury His body, but none of his disciples could approach Pilate to request the body. Though they had the anointing and calling as apostles of our Lord, they didn't have the influence to reach Pilate. It was Joseph of Arimathea who went to see Pilate. For him, it was not a problem. He was properly connected. He was given that influence because of his role in seeing to it that the body of Christ was buried. Thank God Joseph understood this role and fulfilled it. That is how he became relevant in God's project.

God may choose to spare a man's life and allow him to live eighty years in affluence and comfort, all for the purpose of doing one thing for God and humanity. If that person eventually fails to discover and fulfil such a role, he or she has wasted the resources and time provided by God on earth. Joseph discovered his and greatly maximized it.

Joseph of Arimathaea, an honourable counseller, which also waited for the kingdom of God, came, and went in boldly unto Pilate, and craved the body of Jesus. And Pilate marvelled if he were already dead: and calling unto him the centurion, he asked him whether he had been any while dead. And when he knew it of the centurion, he gave the body to Joseph. (Mark 15:43–45)

10.
KEYS TO FUNCTIONING IN YOUR DIVINELY ASSIGNED ROLES

For you to effectively function in your destined roles, there are certain critical issues you must pay attention to. Ignorance of these things can cost the very fulfilment of the divinely assigned roles in which you are meant to function.

The Purpose of God

To properly function in your destined roles, carefully search the purpose of God for your life and for all you dare to do. Our God is a God of purpose; He does nothing without a specific purpose. What we humans often consider a mistake is God's divine arrangement to fulfil His counsel on earth.

You are not a mistake, whether you are a black or white person. You are Nigerian by virtue of God's divine arrangement. There is a reason that

God allowed you to come from Africa, from a specific set of parents, and from the particular tribe you came from. You are not an accident that God is trying to fix up. No, God knew you before you were formed in your mother's womb. God chose you for Himself that He might fulfil His counsel through you.

Discovering the purpose of God for your life is the first key step to fulfilling your divinely assigned roles. It is God's responsibility to design your life and your journey. He did that before your creation. It is your divine responsibility, however, to discover what the Lord designed. The problem often is that men choose to redesign against God's will. Your role is not in the design; it is in the discovery of what has been designed.

In trying to redesign their lives, many people have chosen for themselves good but ungodly paths. No matter who you are or what you can do, God has invested such might and power in you so that you may function and discover your destiny rather than redesign yourself.

Once again, God's role is to design your life and destiny. Yours is to discover what God has designed and function in it. It is the discovery of this design that is called purpose.

Timing

I strongly believe that one of the greatest assets God gave to humanity is time. Time is the only gift that God gave to man equally.

No matter who you are – the richest, the poorest, the busiest, the laziest – everyone has got twenty-four hours of the gift of time each day. The rich do not have more hours than the poor. All are equal.

Time is actually more valuable than money. Time is life. Our capabilities, exploits, and greatness are measured in time. We are where we are today because of what we did yesterday or what was done on our behalf. It is not vanity to say that whatever takes your time takes your life.

For every purpose, there is a right time. When things are done in their proper time, the greatness is overwhelming. It was said concerning the men of Issachar, 'And of the children of Issachar, which were men that had understanding of the times, to know what Israel ought to do; the heads of them were two hundred; and all their brethren were at their commandment' (1 Chron. 12:32).

The men of Issachar were gifted in the understanding of what Israel ought to do, not what

Israel wanted to do. For every vision, there is a time allotted. If you go before that time, you miss the provision of God for the assignment. If you go after that time, you walk in insufficiency, and you struggle in fulfilling the vision. Knowing the timing of God for your life and walking in it is the most appropriate strategy.

Most people grab the understanding of what God wants them to do, but they move ahead before the time God prefers. You must understand what God wants you to do. That is good. But you must also seek to understand His timing for His purpose for your life. That God grants you a revelation of His will for your life today does not necessarily mean the timing is immediate. God often gives visions and revelations ahead of time to enable you to prepare. Unfortunately, people tend to act immediately, at the time of the manifestation of their purpose. This eventually leads to poor performance.

To every thing there is a season, and a time to every purpose under the heaven: A time to be born, and a time to die; a time to plant, and a time to pluck up that which is planted; A time to kill, and a time to heal; a time to break down, and a time to build up; A time to weep, and a time to laugh; a time to mourn, and a time to dance; A time to cast away stones, and a time to gather stones together; a time to embrace, and a time to refrain from embracing; A time to get, and a time to lose; a time to keep, and a time to cast away; A time to rend, and a time to sew; a time to keep silence, and a time to speak; A time to love, and a time to hate; a time of war, and a time of peace. (Eccles. 3:1–8)

Place

Every destiny has a geography. You are a seed of God on earth, and divine design has made you fruitful only on certain soil. The discovery of this will help you greatly when you determine what you see and who sees you. So many destinies struggle for survival because people are wrongly placed for the roles God has called them to fulfil.

The help you need does not come from abroad; it can come only from above. Running helter-skelter will only add to your sorrows and troubles. To be effective in life, you must understand that your destiny has a geography attached. There are chosen places for you at certain times.

There may be a period during which God wants you in one city, and another time during which He wants you in a different city – if He so designs it. It is true that the Lord is your shepherd, but do not go when God is not going with you. Move only when the cloud moves. Let the Word of the Lord be a guide for your life.

Do not forget that God has designed your life, the geography included. Yours is the discovery. You must find out from God where God has chosen for you to dwell. For Abraham, it was a place God showed him (Gen. 12:1). Choose to be where God ordains you to be, and you will see your life blooming.

Elimelech and Naomi made a mistake. They went out of the land where God had planted them, and travelled into another:

Now it came to pass in the days when the judges ruled, that there was a famine in the land. And a certain man of Bethlehemjudah went to sojourn in the country of Moab, he, and his wife, and his two sons. And the name of the man was Elimelech, and the name of his wife Naomi, and the name of his two sons Mahlon and Chilion, Ephrathites of

Bethlehemjudah. And they came into the country of Moab, and continued there.

And Elimelech Naomi's husband died; and she was left, and her two sons. And they took them wives of the women of Moab; the name of the one was Orpah, and the name of the other Ruth: and they dwelled there about ten years. And Mahlon and Chilion died also both of them; and the woman was left of her two sons and her husband. Then she arose with her daughters in law, that she might return from the country of Moab: for she had heard in the country of Moab how that the Lord had visited his people in giving them bread. (Ruth 1:1–6)

So they two went until they came to Bethlehem. And it came to pass, when they were come to Bethlehem, that all the city was moved about them, and they said, Is this Naomi? And she said unto them, Call me not Naomi, call me Mara: for the Almighty hath dealt very bitterly with me. I went out full and the Lord hath brought me home again empty: why then call ye me Naomi, seeing the Lord hath testified against me, and the Almighty hath afflicted me? (Ruth 1:19–21)

People

You cannot function effectively in your role in isolation. You surely will need others. The small intestine, as important as it is in the human body, cannot be the whole body. The body requires all parts in order to be complete. Fulfilling your destiny in isolation is an impossible task for which God has not made provision. God consultated while creating man in Genesis 1:26. Jesus needed at least twelve disciples to fulfil His mandate on earth. You cannot be different. No matter what harm or evil others might cause you, you will still need people to actively function in your role.

God designed our lives in such a way that we would always have reasons to need one another. However, not everybody will be needed for the fulfilment of your roles. Some people may be extremely dangerous, and you will need to avoid them. Some may cause major setbacks, and you do not need them. Some, though evil, may be like Judas Iscariot and push you to the fulfilment of your destiny. You must be prayerful in receiving the people God has made available to you and be sensitive to recognize them when they come. Some may not be dressed in the garments of kings or queens, but inside them are the seeds that will bring forth kings. You may need the other eye to see these.

Just as God will be sending men and women your way, you must not forget that you are a person God has sent to others. Do unto others as you want others to do unto you. This is the summary of the Law and the prophets (Matt. 7:12).

Pray to receive these people. Recognize them as helpers and place them in their right function. Some are sent to you as your financial help – do not place them as counsellors. That is the role for another person or group of people. Some people may require training; they may not be the finished products for the assignment at the time God sends them to you. Do not use them wrongly.

The people God sends to you as a financial help may not appear to be who they are. That does not mean they won't fulfil their role. They carry the potential and power, and they will function properly.

People are not only sent to help you financially or to be counsellors. There are some people God may send your way to pray for you. You may not even know them. Their reward will be commensurate with their faithfulness. If they fail in their place of assignment, they will fail in their reward.

There is the right bricklayer to help you build your house. You will also need the right mechanic and assistant and others as well.

Jesus Christ is our example. He took time to pray for the men He needed to fulfil His assignment on earth. The apostle Peter was illiterate, but he was key in fulfilling the assignment. Judas Iscariot was needed also if the vision was to be fulfilled. You must take time in prayer for your helpers to come to you.

Perhaps the reason you are still struggling is that people who should play certain roles are yet to manifest.

No wonder David was great. He was blessed with men – and not just men, but the right men.

Another important factor is keeping or managing the people God gives you. Many have lost their helpers through carelessness; they are negligent or not concerned about the people God gives them.

David was different. He would go to battle, win, take the spoils, and share with his brethren. He called his men 'brethren'. He was not bossy toward his people; he served them. Those who needed encouragement, he encouraged. He did not become inaccessible – a boss who only gave commands. He was a leader with whom his men could share their burdens. No wonder they jeopardized their lives for him.

Another way that God can bring key people your way are as mentors and fathers in faith who train and equip you for the journey ahead. Mentors are people who are where you desire to be or possess what you desire to possess. Their roles in your life are to make your journey easier and faster. Ignoring or staying distant from them places a major snare on your path.

Ensure that you prayerfully receive the people God brings your way. Be sensitive to recognize them. Allow them to function in their God-sent roles in your life. Maintain a proper relationship with them at all levels.

You must also understand which people you are sent to be with. You may not be sent to all people. Some people have an assignment among the teenagers, some among children, some among the oppressed, some among the poor, some among the aged or the weak. Wherever you are directed, be certain you know who your audience is in the divine counsel of God.

Strategy

God is ever unique in His ways; He does things uniquely. Every assignment, vision, and purpose has its own strategy for fulfilment. The strategy for success for Mr A may not work for Mrs B. Each person must receive from God the strategy for the assignment, vision, and purpose God has given him or her.

King David seemed to understand this well. He consulted God before going to any battle, and if God gave him a go-ahead, King David also received from God the strategy for victory. David would not go into the next battle with the strategy he had used in winning the previous battle, even when it was a God-given strategy. He consulted with God again for a new direction and method. Had he gone in with the previous strategy, he might have failed.

But when the Philistines heard that they had anointed David king over Israel, all the Philistines came up to seek David; and David heard of it, and went down to the hold. The Philistines also came and spread themselves in the valley of Rephaim. And David enquired of the Lord, saying, Shall I go up to the Philistines? wilt thou deliver them into mine hand? And the Lord said unto David, Go up: for I will doubtless deliver the Philistines into thine hand. And David came to Baalperazim, and David smote them there, and said, The Lord hath broken forth upon mine enemies before me, as the breach of waters. Therefore he called the name of that place Baalperazim. And there they left their images, and David and his men burned them. And the Philistines came up yet again, and spread themselves in the valley of Rephaim. And when David enquired of the Lord, he said, Thou shalt not go up; but fetch a compass behind them, and come upon them over against the mulberry trees. And let it be, when thou hearest the sound of a going in the tops of the mulberry trees, that then thou shalt bestir thyself: for then shall the Lord go out before thee, to smite the host of the Philistines. And David did so, as the Lord had commanded him; and smote the Philistines from Geba until thou come to Gazer. (2 Sam. 5:17–25)

David was wise in that he understood that God always has strategies in fulfilling His counsel. Though your vision may be right, if you employ the wrong strategies, you may struggle and crumble. To be effective in your destined role, seek God for the right strategies. God may have a method chosen especially to bless you. If you are ignorant of this method, you may be denied your very opportunity of blessing.

The Measure

We are not equal. We are different and unique in our callings and roles. In our differences, there is a measure of grace and anointing that we all possess so that we may fulfil the counsel of God for our lives.

Biological science reveals that blood, as it is circulated throughout the human body, is not equally distributed. Some parts of the body receive more blood than others. This is because those parts require the extra blood in order to function effectively. Similarly, parts of the body that require less blood will malfunction if more is supplied. This knowledge and understanding is essential as it relates to our destiny.

We all have measures of grace based on the gifts of God on our lives. 'But unto every one of us is given grace according to the measure of the gift of Christ' (Eph. 4:7). In fulfilling your destiny, it is good to have an understanding of the measure of grace and anointing upon your life. This helps you stay focused and discourages you from exhibiting envy, jealousy, and distractions.

There is a measure of God's grace upon every life, based on the assignment and calling of God. Stay within the measure and fulfil your destined roles. Do not be a competitor envying others who are simply operating in the measure of God for their lives. We must be conscious that, as in a biological system, we all must locate our positions in the body of Christ and function appropriately. This is essential for growth and fulfilment of the counsel of God on earth. It must be done in love and understanding, not in envy and jealousy. You must not forget we are one body in Christ Jesus.

Potential

Your potential is a gift from God for you to take into your future. Everyone has been given several abilities. Though the measures may differ, you surely possess something that is essential for the fulfilment of God's purpose and counsel for your life.

Your potential is God's gift of abilities that are yet to be revealed or manifested. There is something in you that is yet to be revealed or known. Your potential is what you can do that you have not yet done. It is the power of God at work on you yet to be manifested.

Potential is what the earth earnestly expects to see. It is the dream in your heart, the vision you are carrying. Your dream waits to be enabled by your potential in a way that gives uniqueness to your calling and to your destiny. The full expression of your potential breeds fulfilment of your life assignment. You can be that thing that God has revealed you are if you would only add effect and commitment and allow your potential to manifest.

Your potential is given to you because of what you have been designed to do by God. The power at work in you is there because of what it is meant to accomplish in your life. You may never come into the land of your fulfilment if you fail to recognize and use your potential. Your recognition and use of your abilities enable you to function at your maximum.

A borrowed strength is an inherent weakness. Most of what you seek help for is what you can do and achieve. Your abilities may be crude at the beginning, but training will refine them.

Many youths today need to be encouraged to look for more from within, for what is not seen without may be seen within. They would accomplish their dreams faster if they looked within to see that the omnipotent Judge did not create them as empty beings without worth who must depend on others to survive. We would all be surprised to see the vast amount of gold deposited in us by the Creator of the universe, if only we looked within.

It is amazing that people have within them more treasures than those they are waiting to get by depending on others. Those who truly fail are those who came to earth to enjoy the labour of faithful people without making their own contributions. The earth is rich and willing to assist anyone who is desirous to make our home a better place. Certainly heaven will one day ask us to give account of what we have done with what was given unto us.

11.
THE COST OF FULFILLING DIVINELY ASSIGNED ROLES

Discover Your Role

The first step to fulfilling divinely assigned roles is to discover the role to fulfil. You cannot fulfil the role you do not know and understand.

It is not sufficient to have a glimpse or an idea of what the role is. You must seek to understand, in detail, who you are in God's counsel and what role you have been assigned by God to fulfil on earth. Without the appropriate understanding, the goal of fulfilment is a mirage.

Many people have acted upon or fulfilled other people's roles because they are ignorant of who they are. We must, if we desire satisfaction in life, seek to discover the role assigned to us. Then we must be willing to fulfil it.

The best way to discover your role is to ask the One who made you – God. He alone can tell in detail who you are and why you exist. If you seek God with all your heart, you will find Him.

People frequently complain that they are not sure God will speak to them or that they won't be able to hear Him if He does speak. The truth is, if you are a child of God, you should be able to hear from God. He speaks to us in different ways – through His Word; by the Holy Spirit in our spirits; by prophecy, vision, trances, and dreams; and at times through situations and circumstances. It can simply be a knowing inside of you.

In order to be a child of God, you must be born again. In other words, you must believe in your heart that Jesus Christ died for your sin on the cross of Calvary and rose from the dead. You must confess with your mouth that He is Lord (Rom. 10).

So watch which method God uses to communicate to you. You will surely find Him if you seek Him with all your heart.

Empowerment

God's revelation of who you are and what you are to do is only the starting point to fulfilling His purpose and counsel in your life. Knowing this is not sufficient if you are to fulfil your roles effectively. You need to be empowered for what you are called to do. The church today is filled with people who are qualified, but they are not prepared for what God has called them to do.

Many people cannot climb to the pinnacle of relevance, not because they were not ordained to, but because they are unprepared for the will and counsel of God. They are lazy and undisciplined. They lack of perseverance. These are some of the key hindrances that keep people from fulfilling great dreams.

Today, youths with great potential are wasting away, failing in their pursuit of destiny, not because they do not have desire or will, but because the corresponding inner energy to drive them is missing. We all need this inner energy called empowerment. What physical energy is to the human body, inner energy is to our destiny. We cannot drive much without it. Its absence makes us dreamers; its presence, achievers.

Empowerment is to destiny what fuel is to a car. You need all-round empowerment to drive your dream to reality.

There are five key areas of empowerment – physical, emotional, spiritual, mental, and financial.

Physical Empowerment

Our human body is one of the most precious gifts given to us by the omniscient Judge of the universe. We cannot live on the planet without this body suit; it's our legal entry to the earth. Damage to it can cut our lives short before our time is up. Good maintenance, therefore, contributes greatly to our living effectively on earth. It provides us with more opportunities to fulfil our roles in life.

Physical empowerment speaks of the upkeep of our bodies. Take a warm bath daily. Eat good food, including fruits and vegetables in the right proportion. Exercise your body to keep fit. Take adequate rest. At times, fast, which will go a long way towards keep you physically fit. Consult a dietician, who can recommend a food timetable convenient for your pocketbook. Avoid alcohol, marijuana, and cigarettes. Their side effects on your body are poisonous and will not help your life.

You are unique. You must treat yourself that way. Dress neatly. Keep your environment clean and tidy. You can avoid unnecessary diseases that way. Keep your nails neat and clean and well-trimmed. Do not put on dirty clothes.

All of these practices will help you stay healthy. It is the desire of God that you should be strong and healthy. Your physical empowerment is essential to the fulfilment of your divinely assigned roles.

Emotional Empowerment

Every human experiences emotion. Some have described emotion as energy in motion (in other words, e-motion). The dictionary defines emotion as connecting to human feelings – the way people feel. Many destinies have been ruined by improper management of emotion. Many great leaders and their potential have been buried because their emotions became their leaders. Others, in ignoring or not properly using their emotions, have denied themselves great blessings and opportunities. Moses eventually became a victim of unmanaged emotion. Samson was weak emotionally. David had a similar problem. Gehazi is not left out.

Our emotions, if not well managed, can bring us to a place of shame. Likewise, if properly channelled, they can bring us to a place of honour. Great leaders are people who understand the correct use of emotion. They do not make decisions from an emotional standpoint; rather, they make decisions from the standpoint of conviction. To be effective and strong in fulfilling your destiny, you cannot ignore the fact that you have emotions. You must choose to properly master and control your emotions so they can function when and where they are needed.

Spiritual Empowerment

This is the most crucial kind of empowerment. Every physical manifestation is the shadow of real spiritual substance. Like the saying goes, 'We cannot travel without when we are still standing within.' There is always a corresponding change in the physical realm to reflect a change in the spiritual realm.

Unfortunately, people believe that only those called to the pulpit ministry need spiritual empowerment. No, this is not true. Those in the pulpit ministries need it, but others also need it. The true measure of your strength is determined by your spiritual strength. True and genuine covering is secure over every destiny through proper and correct spiritual empowerment. Spiritual empowerment is enriched when your salvation experience is genuine and your fellowship with the Lord is continual.

If you are thoroughly empowered spiritually, your manifestation will be great in the physical. Every physical position and place has a corresponding spiritual standing. If you refuse adequate spiritual empowerment, you will become ineffective for your destiny manifestation, irrespective of your calling and assignment.

To receive genuine spiritual empowerment, certain things must be properly put in place:

- *Genuine Salvation:* Salvation is genuine when you believe in your heart that Jesus Christ is the son of God and that He died on the cross of Calvary for your sins. You must make confession of this belief as well (Rom. 10:9–10). When you are saved, or born again, you are delivered from the kingdom of darkness and brought into the kingdom of light, which is Jesus Christ. You are no longer under the control and leadership of Satan; neither are you under the control of sin. You are now under the control and leadership of God by His son, Jesus Christ, through the Holy Spirit.

Genuine salvation means you are saved from something negative (not by your power) into something positive.

Salvation is the work of grace. It is earned by faith and not by works. If you are not sure of your salvation, it is better to accept it by believing the Word of the Lord. Because of His love for you, He sent His only begotten Son, Jesus Christ, to die on the cross for your sins (John 3:16). Confess with your mouth today that Jesus is Lord and your Saviour, and you will be saved.

- *Right Fellowship:* Believers in the kingdom of God must be careful about which fellowships and organizations they submit themselves to. This is because what you are joined to determines what happens in your life. You should not join a church because it is very close to your house or because it is where your great-grandfather attended. The church you go to and the leadership you submit to will determine greatly the kind of spiritual flow that will be channelled into your life. Followers do not become what their leaders teach, but who their leaders are. So in choosing a fellowship or church, you must be guided prayerfully.

This is not applicable to church attendance alone; it applies also to friendship associations and groups you might join. Many people, in joining themselves to the wrong company, lose their lives and their destinies. Judas Iscariot joined himself to the betrayers and was taken into error. Beware of wrong company.

- *Correct Mentoring:* Every great tree will first be planted in the nursery before being transplanted to its final site. This is to allow for good and proper grooming of the growing tree. This exercise is needed to regulate the amount of heat, sunlight, water, and atmosphere necessary for the normal growth of the plant.

A mentor is someone who possesses a large percentage of the qualities you desire to possess, who knows what you do not know, or has been where you desire to be and can guide you along the right path through his or her acquired knowledge and experience. Many destinies are slow in making impact because they are not properly mentored. Many people who could have become champions are now long forgotten because the arrows of their destinies were not discovered. Had they been blessed with appropriate mentoring, they could have hit the real target.

When we submit to appropriate mentoring, our journeys are accelerated. It is an advantage to have the opportunity to learn from the errors of others and hence avoid falling into the same errors. Correct mentoring introduces the correct spirit. Correct mentoring creates platforms for manifestation and opens you up to godly inheritances in the spirit. It brings covering over destiny and protects your destiny from unnecessary satanic access. When you are properly mentored, you are properly guided and trained for the work you are called to do.

- *Personal Relationship with the Father:* True spiritual empowerment is not complete without a personal relationship with God. Although salvation is the first step to true spiritual empowerment, it is not the only step. You must work out your salvation with trembling and fear.

  Your personal relationship with the Father is the place of deep meditation upon the Word of God. Fasting and prayer and fellowship with the Holy Spirit are inestimable channels to unquenchable spiritual empowerment. This truth cannot be substituted for any other. If you are to be strong spiritually, the personal relationship you have with God is essential. It enables you to know more of God and of His ways. It keeps you from the path of distraction and destruction.

- *Purity and Holiness:* For your spiritual empowerment to be real, you need to flee every appearance of evil in thought, word, and deed. Sin and impurity are means of weakening spiritual strength and capability. No matter how much you fast and pray, you will be greatly hindered when sin dwells in your life. Though there may be passion when you fall into error, you must immediately confess your sins and repent of them (1 John 1:9). If we confess our sins, God is faithful and just; He will forgive us and cleanse us from all unrighteousness.

You must live in complete and instant obedience to God's Word and instructions. Stay away from every form of sin in order to enjoy thorough and deep spiritual empowerment. Spiritual empowerment enables you to function effectively in the divinely assigned role God has chosen you to function in —ministry, governance, or family. Your spiritual empowerment will enrich every other empowerment.

- *Use of Resource Materials:* There is no baton of life you need that someone else does not hold. You may not be able to access every resource personally through physical contact, but you can access them through books (printed or on tape) and, with the advancement in technology, through the Internet. To be complete in spiritual empowerment, you will need the contributions of others whom God has divinely positioned to be blessings to your life and journey. Some of these people may no longer be alive, but their words are available to be relevant to what God is calling you to do.

It is practically impossible for you to be a leader without being a reader. Every leader is the sum total of the contributions of other leaders he or she has chosen to receive. The greater the contributions you receive, the greater the impact you can make. Each of us, by redemption, has an opportunity to be a key leader in the area of our callings. We determine what impact we make by our level of empowerment. The greater the empowerment, the greater our impact becomes. It is with the same measure that it shall be measured back to you.

Mental Empowerment

You need mental empowerment to ensure relevance in your divinely assigned role. Nothing can take the role of education and training on earth, either formal or informal. In most cases, both are required for you to be relevant.

You cannot be born an architect. You need to be trained as one. Most inabilities or incompetencies are traceable to lack of training. Directly or indirectly, training is one of the legs on which you must walk to greatness. Irrespective of where you have been called to function in life, you can never diminish yourself by receiving training. If you are called to be a lawyer, then choose to stand out. Do postgraduate studies and join relevant associations that can position you for the greatness you have dreamed of.

You should not pursue certificates for promotion alone, however. They will eventually not be helpful in becoming the best God wants you to be. If you need to return to an apprentice state, put in the time and learn, prior qualifications notwithstanding. If the person training you is lesser in any respect, submit yourself and you will see yourself glowing. Choose to learn rather than to earn, and you will eventually employ those who made the choice to earn. If you have your first degree, what is stopping you from going for a second? Choose empowerment, and your opportunities will expand.

Financial Empowerment

In the fulfilment of every vision and role, money plays a vital part. From the distribution of tracts to holding a crusade, money is key. Hence, ignorance of financial management will cause major trouble to anyone who desires to implement a vision.

Still, no matter how relevant money is, it must not take the place of God and His purpose for your life. Money is one of the tools God blesses you with to help you function effectively in your life journey and assignment. You must not see money as the ultimate but as a tool to work with.

Certain things determine how much empowerment you have access to financially. Some of these include:

- *The Nature of your Assignment:* God makes provision only for vision. Every token God supplies is for a particular assignment or need – yours as an individual included. Money may come to another person rather than to you, because of the assignment God has for that person, which requires more money than yours.

- *Your Attitude about Money:* The way you interpret the meaning and purpose of money can greatly determine how much of it you will have.

- *What you Do with Money:* The things you do with money can determine if more money will come to you or if money will move away from you. In other words, when thinking about spending or investing money, do you use that money for eternal purposes or solely for selfish purposes?

- *Your Faithfulness with Money:* If you are not faithful with unrighteous Mammon, who will commit to your trust the true riches? Are you faithful in paying tithes? Do you obey God and do what He wants you to do with the money committed to your trust?

- *Your Knowledge about Money:* This can also determine, to a great extent, what becomes of your financial empowerment.

Focus

Focus is part of the price to pay to function effectively in your divinely assigned roles. Nobody gets things done when he or she is multisighted. Every man of exploit is a man of one thing. The apostle Paul said, 'This one thing I do' (Phil. 3:13). There will be many things that appeal to you, but you must discover one thing that summarizes your whole being. When people lose their vision, they lose their lives as well. When people are distracted from their vision, their lives become scattered.

The greatest weapon of the Enemy is to cause us to lose focus on our assignment. Once focus is lost, energy is lost, strength becomes weak, and purpose is meaningless. The apostle Peter would not have sunk in Matthew 14:25–30 if his focus had not been distracted away from the Master. Even in science, when a lens is used to trap light to a particular point on a paper, the paper will eventually ignite.

A loss of focus is a just little less destructive than a life without vision. Being a person of all is being a person of none. To be relevant in your assignment, identify with what God has called you to do and summarize your life. Give it all that is required; do not be distracted by the success others are having. Everyone is working by his or her own timing, and that timing differs. What you achieve at this time, I may achieve at another time.

What is important is discovering what you are supposed to do. Then you must know how you are supposed to do it, when you are supposed to do it, where you are supposed to do it, and for whom you are supposed to do it (Matt.14:25–30).

Discipline

Nature has not given an opportunity to any person to climb the ladder of true success if that person has not learned the culture of self-discipline. We are not permitted, by divine mandate, to become relevant if we have not learned to discipline ourselves.

Self-discipline is the measure you place upon yourself to enable you to improve your way of life and achieve your goals. Anybody who desires to become great in life without discipline is only a dreamer who may not see reality.

Many youths today are dreamers with empty realities. Their dreams are not genuine, because they refuse to discipline themselves to accomplish those dreams. Discipline will enable you to deny yourself pleasures that can distract you from your dreams. It is discipline that keeps you awake while others are sleeping. It is discipline that enables you to invest your time in what makes your life. Discipline enables you to put off habits that are pleasant to the body but distracting to your vision. Discipline enables you to keep quiet when you should, and listen rather than being a talkative person. It enables you to plan effectively and to pursue your vision with passion. Without discipline, your dream will remain a dream, and your labour will be unnoticed.

It is discipline that brings the worth out of the waste; it is discipline that keeps you going. You need discipline, either self-imposed or learned through training. Discipline is essential to the achievement of your dream.

Each calling, assignment, and vision requires a corresponding measure of discipline. The discipline an athlete needs to triumph, a politician may not need. The discipline a university undergraduate needs to become a celebrity in his or her department, a singer may not need. So search out disciplinary measures corresponding to the assignment God has given to you and stick to them.

Study carefully those who are ahead of you, those who have made great success in the same field of assignment into which God has called you. Find out what discipline they imposed upon themselves before they could rise. Make a study of at least ten such persons and note additional information or disciplines you need to know. Keep to your path and you will rise. Discipline will take away from your life the additional weight that can hinder you from running the race that is set before you.

Wherefore seeing we also are compassed about with so great a cloud of witnesses, let us lay aside every weight, and the sin which doth so easily beset us, and let us run with patience the race that is set before us, Looking unto Jesus the author and finisher of our faith; who for the joy that was set before him endured the cross, despising the shame, and is set down at the right hand of the throne of God. (Heb. 12:1–2)

I therefore so run, not as uncertainly; so fight I, not as one that beateth the air: But I keep under my body, and bring *it* into subjection: lest that by any means, when I have preached to others, I myself should be a castaway. (1 Cor. 9:26–27)

Courage

We all need courage to reach our goals and to finish our tasks. Often we are behind the reality of what God wants us to be because of our lack of courage. You must develop the courage to keep going no matter how tough the journey seems to be.

You need the courage to say yes when you should and to say no when it is appropriate. You need courage to keep going when you meet fallen heroes on your path. You will surely have sufficient reasons to be discouraged or complacent and to discontinue your journey. It takes courage to keep going. Courage is to a human being what food is to the hungry, what clothing is to nakedness. It gives warmth and vitality. Courage opens you to the victory and reveals to you your true identity as an image of God. Courage tells you it is possible. It gives a refreshing breath and opens your eyes to promise and to the God of the promise.

Many cannot start the journey at all. They wait for pleasant circumstances before they are willing to start. 'He that observeth the wind shall not sow' (Eccles. 11:4). It takes courage to believe God despite circumstances. Some start but cannot continue; they had courage but did not continue in it. Some start but arrived at a false destination. Initial success went to their heads. Yet others start and, as though they are still starting, break new ground every day for the Lord.

For Joshua to be effective in his destiny assignment, all God told him was to be strong and be of good courage (Josh. 1). For Jesus to finish well, He needed courage to endure the cross and to despise the shame for the joy that was set before him (Heb. 12:2).

On your way to the top, you might encounter sufficient reasons why you should not continue. There may be times when it seems all the demons in hell have the address of your home. It takes courage at such moments to keep going. Even when you have achieved much, it takes courage to achieve more. Courage is built from God's promise for your life, the understanding of who you are in God, and the knowledge and understanding of God's commitment to your life.

Most Christians are conscious of the commitment of the Devil to their lives. They understand what the Devil can do and what the Devil is doing. But they understand little about the commitment of God to their lives. This further weakens their courage.

It was courage that made Joshua and Caleb declare their ability in God to possess their possessions. It was what they saw through courage that made them declare their victory. When courage is absent, defeat is in view. If you have not been achieving much for God recently, check if you have sufficient courage to dare more.

Part III Summary

- God does not provide for what He has not called for.
- Every opportunity of life is simply a platform for fulfilling divinely assigned roles.

- Every great and promising destiny has a price.
- No one fulfils destiny by mere wishing.
- Recognizing divine opportunities enables fulfilment of divinely assigned roles.

Part III Questions

- What opportunity do you have that can aid you in fulfilling divinely assigned roles?
- What opportunity do you believe, if attained, will further help you fulfil your divinely assigned roles?
- What preparation are you making to qualify yourself for the opportunities stated above?
- What do you think you must do, or do more, to enable you to function effectively in your divinely assigned roles?
- What must you reduce, take away, or go away from to enable you to fulfil your divinely assigned roles?

PART IV

At the end of this section, you will have an understanding of the following:

- Likely hindrances to fulfilling divinely assigned roles
- Categories of men in relation to divinely assigned roles
- Guides to fulfilling divinely assigned roles.

Tomorrow – men accomplish nothing in the world.

The heights by great men reached and kept were not attained by sudden flight, but they while their companions slept, were toiling upward in the night.

—Henry Wadsworth Longfellow

If you choose to seek and do God's will, then be assured all things will work together for your good.

—OluwaFemi Lanre Oke

12.
UNDERSTANDING LIKELY HINDRANCES TO FULFILLING DIVINELY ASSIGNED ROLES

Sin

Sin is a major obstacle and stumbling block to great would-be destinies that never arrive. Many of our generation would have been giants of the Lord like Samson, but they fell just as Samson fell on the lap of Delilah. Theft, bribery, exaggeration, and lies, among other things, can greatly hinder a visionary from achieving his or her dreams.

Sin is a divider. It reduces the strength of a person to nothing. It opens the door to the Enemy so the Enemy can destroy. Sin is the elder brother of Satan. The Devil is harmless to a Christian without sin. Every giant strife of the Devil comes after a door has been opened by sin. No person who desires to be an agent of change in his or her generation for the Lord would do well living in sin.

In his counsel, Pastor E. A. Adeboye, the general overseer of the Redeemed Christian Church of God worldwide, says, 'Sin is the only thing that can separate a Christian from the presence of God.' To Pastor Joe Jacobs, a senior pastor in Christ Apostolic Church, sin is a no-go area if you want to be an ambassador of change in your generation. 'You cannot go further in life with sin in your life,' says Bishop Francis Wale Oke, the president of Sword of the Spirit Ministries worldwide. The presence of sin is all the Devil needs to access a Christian. Thanks be to the Lord who has given us victory over sin: 'But now being made free from sin, and become servants to God, ye have your fruit unto holiness, and the end everlasting life' (Rom. 6:22).

Ignorance

Ignorance is another key factor that hinders people from fulfilling their divinely assigned roles in God – ignorance of who they are in Christ, of what God has made available to them, of what they are on earth, and of the commitment of God to them. There is no mountain before us more insurmountable than ignorance.

Our problems are as big as what we do not know. As a matter of fact, every human being on earth is a combination of two things: what he or she knows and what he or she does not know. You are where you are today because of these two factors. The greater your knowledge of the truth, the greater the freedom you enjoy. Another word for ignorance is *darkness*. The extent of your darkness is determined by the amount of light (knowledge of the truth) you can access.

God says, 'My people are destroyed for the lack of knowledge: because thou has rejected knowledge, I will also reject thee, that thou shalt be no priest to me: seeing thou has forgotten the law of thy God, I will also forgot thy children' (Hos. 4:6). For rejecting or refusing to pursue knowledge, God is willing to refuse to allow His people to become leaders. How much leadership and influence you have will therefore greatly be determined by how much you know. The more you know, the greater your leadership capacity will be.

Among other things, as one who would fulfil God's counsel, you must seek to know in detail the following:

- The will of God
- The Word of God
- The way of God

Your knowledge in these areas is essential for your life. 'And beside this, giving all diligence, add to your faith virtue; and to virtue knowledge' (2 Pet. 1:5). 'For if these things be in you, and abound, they make you that ye shall neither be barren nor unfruitful in the knowledge of our Lord Jesus Christ' (2 Pet. 1:8).

Wrong Covering

Wrong covering has to do with mentoring or guiding. Many lives have lost fulfilment because they are under the wrong spiritual covering. People have lost their vision, focus, and passion by following a leader who is not suitable as a covering for their lives. As great and important as spiritual cover is to a destiny, the wrong one is worse. So you must seek God diligently to guide you appropriately.

Wrong Beliefs

Every man and woman is a product of his or her beliefs. Your actions correspond to what you believe. That is why it is said that the environment in which you grow determines a lot about you. Your environment contributes greatly to your belief system.

A belief is not an idea that a person possesses. A belief is an idea that possesses a person. When your belief is wrong, your actions and decisions are wrong; your life hence becomes wrong.

Check your beliefs with the Word of God. A partial wrong belief can do you great harm. Undo every wrong belief that tradition, culture, and human opinions have implanted in your life. Sow the timeless seeds of truth instead.

Wrong Confession

'Of the abundance of the heart his mouth speaketh' (Luke 6:45). There is a correlation between what we say and what future lies ahead of us. Jesus taught this in Mark 11:22–25, emphasizing what to say and how to say it. The book of Proverbs speaks a lot about the wisdom of speaking correctly.

To enjoy a life full of blessings, cultivate the habit of speaking your faith and not your fears. Words are powerful; they are seeds. They bring to you the harvest of whatever you keep saying. Whatever you do not want to see in your life, do not say with your mouth.

Most Christians have not seen their long-awaited help because of their wrong confessions. Whatever you repeatedly say has spiritual potency that manifests in your life. 'Death and life *are* in the power of the tongue: and they that love it shall eat the fruit thereof' (Prov. 18:21).

Do not confess what you see that you do not want. Confess what you want to see that you have not seen. There is power in your tongue to bring into the seen realms what is trapped in the unseen. Your words are vehicles; use them properly.

Wrong Habits

Bad or wrong habits are also critical in hindering the fulfilment of God's counsel. Whatever you practice continually for at least four days becomes a habit. A habit once formed becomes, gradually, part of your character.

Bad habits like laziness (not doing), procrastination (doing later what you can do now), and slothfulness (starting a work and not finishing it) will greatly hinder you from fulfilling your destiny. To undo a bad habit, you must consciously identify the habit you want to change and determine to change it with its antidote. Rather than do your work later, tell yourself you will do it now. Never put off till later what you can do now. Don't find an excuse, no matter how genuine, as a reason for not getting things done.

Those who will make their marks in life are those who are willing, against all odds, to fulfil their God-given mandates. You are one of them. Laziness is one of the deadliest obstacles that can hinder you from achieving your life goals. So do not give in to it. Every great hero, living or dead, has a lifestyle free of laziness. After discovering the path that God has chosen for you to tread, prepare yourself and work; that is the secret. Deal now with every habit that hinders you from reaching your goals.

Wrong Priorities

One of the essential laws of life is the law of priorities. Matthew 6:33 says, 'But seek first His kingdom and His righteousness' (KJV). You are not just to seek the kingdom of God – you are to seek it first. This is the law of priority. You must place your priorities in accordance with God's will and plans for your life.

Working and living with the perspective of God will greatly assist you in placing your priorities correctly. Wrong priorities can lead to unnecessary loss of energy, focus, and resources. When priorities are not right, we risk taking the wrong steps and actions, and our destinies are hindered.

Wrong Company

Your friends are the true identity of who you are and what can become of you. You can be greatly influenced by your associations. It has been said that you are the sum total of the books you read and the friends you keep. Wrong associations attract wrong flow into your life. When you keep wrong company, you pollute yourself, your vision, and your life.

King Saul was a victim of wrong company. He surrounded himself with people who led him astray. King Solomon was another example. He married wives who took him far away from God.

You may not be able to choose your brothers or sisters, but you sure can choose your friends and associates. If you have been lured into a wrong relationship, consciously or unconsciously, I appeal to you to be bold and come out of it. It will help you more than you can ever imagine.

A man's friends are a reflection of who he is. Your future can be accurately predicted by the kind of people you join yourself with. In a way, you can change your life if you change your associates. You are as strong as the people who surround you. Why not make them the right ones?

Wrong Thoughts

'For as he thinketh in his heart, so is he' (Prov. 23:7). If you are to change a person's life, you must change his or her thoughts. You are your thoughts.

The reason so many people are backwards in life is because their thoughts are backwards; they are consumed with thoughts of past events and negative things, and hence they are negative. Like the saying goes, 'You cannot travel within and be stagnant without.'

Your words are the reflection of your thoughts (Matt. 11:36), and your future a product of your words (Prov. 18:21). Good luck cannot be your portion when your thoughts are continually about bad luck. It is true – you may not rise beyond your thoughts.

Every divine visitation is communicated from the spirit to the mind for processing. If your thoughts have been programmed only to evaluate negative ideas, you will not be able to achieve anything positive. Many people would have been heroes but have been greatly hindered by their negative thoughts. They allowed the Devil to preoccupy their minds with mundane things – care of the world and prevailing negative circumstances.

Worry is a by-product of wrong thinking. It compounds trouble rather than alleviating it. To live a victorious life, think of the solution. Think of the Word of God. Think of His promises, revelations, and prophecies. Think of the possibilities and opportunities ahead. Think of the change you desire, and keep confessing the change. You will see your life drastically changing for the best.

Stop worrying. Rather, sing praises and hymns to the One who alone can meet your needs. Write out on a sheet of paper what your worries are and present them to the Lord in prayer. Believe He has heard you and answered you, then praise Him for it. Now think the answers to your prayers and confess them. Enjoy unlimited victory.

13.
CATEGORIES OF PEOPLE IN RELATION TO DIVINELY ASSIGNED ROLES

And the children of Israel did evil again in the sight of the Lord; and the Lord delivered them into the hand of the Philistines forty years. And there was a certain man of Zorah, of the family of the Danites, whose name was Manoah; and his wife was barren, and bare not. And the angel of the Lord appeared unto the woman, and said unto her, Behold now, thou art barren, and bearest not: but thou shalt conceive, and bear a son. Now therefore beware, I pray thee, and drink not wine nor strong drink, and eat not any unclean thing: For, lo, thou shalt conceive, and bear a son; and no razor shall come on his head: for the child shall be a Nazarite unto God from the womb: and he shall begin to deliver Israel out of the hand of the Philistines. (Judg. 13:1–5)

There are seven categories of people in relation to divinely assigned roles. The first are those who do not understand or know their roles. Hence they do nothing and make no impact. They only live and die. An example is Methuselah: 'And Methuselah lived an hundred eighty and seven years, and begat Lamech. And Methuselah lived after he begat Lamech seven hundred eighty and two years, and begat sons and daughters: And all the days of Methuselah were nine hundred sixty and nine years: and he died' (Gen. 5:25–27).

The second category are the people who do not understand clearly their roles and hence play another person's role. An example is Eve:

Now the serpent was more subtil than any beast of the field which the Lord God had made. And he said unto the woman, Yea, hath God said, Ye shall not eat of every tree of the garden? And the woman said unto the serpent, We may eat of the fruit of the trees of the garden: But of the fruit of the tree which is in the midst of the garden, God hath said, Ye shall not eat of it, neither shall ye touch it, lest ye die. And the serpent said unto the woman, Ye shall not surely die: For God doth know that in the day ye eat thereof, then your eyes shall be opened, and ye shall be as gods, knowing good and evil. And when the woman saw that the tree was good for food, and that it was pleasant to the eyes, and a tree to be desired to make one wise, she took of the fruit thereof, and did eat, and gave also unto her husband with her; and he did eat. (Gen. 3:1–6)

Eve played the role of Adam, and it landed her in trouble. She was not supposed to make such a decision without the consent of her husband. She did not understand clearly what her role was and thus took on another person's role.

The third category are those who understand their roles but do nothing about it. An example is Eli:

And the Lord said to Samuel, Behold, I will do a thing in Israel, at which both the ears of every one that heareth it shall tingle. In that day I will perform against Eli all things which I have spoken concerning his house: when I begin, I will also make an end. For I have told him that I will judge his house for ever for the iniquity which he knoweth; because his sons made themselves vile, and he restrained them not. (1 Sam. 3:11–13)

Eli was judged for the sin he knew. His sons made themselves vile, and he did not restrain them. Despite the warning, all Eli did was ask the Lord to do as it pleased Him. He did not take steps to make amends. Such people, the Bible says, will be beaten with many stripes (Luke 12:47).

The fourth category are those who understand their roles, start them, but do not finish. An example is Samson. Samson's birth was unique; it was predicted by an angel of the Lord, and a caution was given to his parents about how to take care of the baby when he was born. His purpose were stated before his birth: he was to deliver his people from the oppression of the Philistines. He did a little towards that goal, but he couldn't deliver his clan before he died. Although he understood his role in life, and he started to fulfil it, he was hindered from completing the task.

And she said, The Philistines be upon thee, Samson. And he awoke out of his sleep, and said, I will go out as at other times before, and shake myself. And he wist not that the LORD was departed from him. But the Philistines took him and put out his eyes and brought him down to

Gaza, and bound him with fetters of brass: and he did grind in the prison house. (Judg. 16:20–21)

The fifth category are those who understand their roles, start the work, almost finish it, but do not finish. An example is Moses:

Now Moses kept the flock of Jethro his father in law, the priest of Midian: and he led the flock to the backside of the desert, and came to the mountain of God, even to Horeb. And the angel of the Lord appeared unto him in a flame of fire out of the midst of a bush: and he looked, and, behold, the bush burned with fire, and the bush was not consumed. And Moses said, I will now turn aside, and see this great sight, why the bush is not burnt. And when the Lord saw that he turned aside to see, God called unto him out of the midst of the bush, and said, Moses, Moses. And he said, Here am I. And he said, Draw not nigh hither: put off thy shoes from off thy feet, for the place whereon thou standest is holy ground. Moreover he said, I am the God of thy father, the God of Abraham, the God of Isaac, and the God of Jacob. And Moses hid his face; for he was afraid to look upon God. And the Lord said, I have surely seen the affliction of my people which are in Egypt, and have heard their cry by reason of their taskmasters; for I know their sorrows; And I am come down to deliver them out of the hand of the Egyptians, and to bring them up out of that land unto a good land and a large, unto a land flowing with milk and honey; unto the place of the Canaanites, and the Hittites, and the Amorites, and the Perizzites, and the Hivites, and the Jebusites. Now therefore, behold, the cry of the children of Israel is come unto me: and I have also seen the oppression wherewith the Egyptians oppress them. Come now therefore, and I will send thee unto Pharaoh, that thou mayest bring forth my people the children of Israel out of Egypt. (Exod. 3:1–10)

The calling and assignment of Moses were made clear right from the beginning of his journey. He was to deliver the children of Israel from the oppression of the Egyptians and lead them into the land that the Lord had sworn to their fathers, the land flowing with milk and honey.

Moses was a man who did very well but never got to his destination. He laboured, almost got there, but never did. Many heroes fall under similar challenges: they have a bright beginning, do great exploits, almost get to their destinations, but never do.

Furthermore the Lord was angry with me for your sakes, and sware that I should not go over Jordan, and that I should not go in unto that good land, which the Lord thy God giveth thee for an inheritance: But I must die in this land, I must not go over Jordan: but ye shall go over, and possess that good land. (Deut. 4:21–22)

Moses was unable to enter into the Promised Land. What can hinder you from getting there?

The sixth category are those who understood their roles, started the process of fulfilling them, and finished. An example is Paul:

And I said, Who art thou, Lord? And he said, I am Jesus whom thou persecutest. But rise, and stand upon thy feet: for I have appeared unto thee for this purpose, to make thee a minister and a witness both of these things which thou hast seen, and of those things in the which I will appear unto thee; Delivering thee from the people, and from the Gentiles, unto whom now I send thee, To open their eyes, and to turn them from darkness to light, and from the power of Satan unto God, that they may receive forgiveness of sins, and inheritance among them which are sanctified by faith that is in me. Whereupon, O king Agrippa, I was not disobedient unto the heavenly vision. (Acts 26:15–19)

For I am now ready to be offered, and the time of my departure is at hand. I have fought a good fight, I have finished my course, I have kept the faith. (2 Tim. 4:6–7)

Paul was a man who had understanding of his callings and missions here on earth. He did not do otherwise; he was obedient to the heavenly calling. Though there were distractions, opposition, limitations, and hindrances, all timed out to be good for him. Irrespective of what happened to him, he overcame and finished his task.

Paul was a highly determined man who would not take no for an answer when it should be yes. He was discouraged from travelling at one point for fear of opposition, but he went. He was more concerned about the will of God than he was about comfort and pleasure. No wonder he finished strong. He wrote two-thirds of the New Testament.

What would you allow to hinder you from fulfilling your destiny? Laziness, procrastination, comfort, pleasure, opinions of men – what excuse would you give? Paul is good role model. Ask yourself, do you think you would finish your course on earth? The Lord who helped Paul would also help you!

The seventh category are those who fulfil negative roles. Examples are Pharaoh and Judas Iscariot.

For the scripture saith unto Pharaoh, Even for this same purpose have I raised thee up, that I might shew my power in thee, and that my name might be declared throughout all the earth. (Rom. 9:17)

When Jesus had thus said, he was troubled in spirit, and testified, and said, Verily, verily, I say unto you, that one of you shall betray me. Then the disciples looked one on another, doubting of whom he spake. Now there was leaning on Jesus' bosom one of his disciples, whom Jesus loved. Simon Peter therefore beckoned to him, that he should ask who it should be of whom he spake. He then lying on Jesus' breast saith unto him, Lord, who is it? Jesus answered, He it is, to whom I shall give a sop, when I have dipped it. And when he had dipped the sop, he gave it to Judas Iscariot, the son of Simon. (John 13:21–26)

Part IV Summary

- Every great destiny attracts opposition.
- You can determine how great God will make you.
- Opposition is not meant to frighten you but to strengthen you.
- You are what you allow life to make you.
- Being focused will help you greatly in fulfilling your God-given assignment.

Part IV Questions

- What, in your own opinion, has been a major hindrance to you in discovering and fulfilling your divinely assigned roles?
- What are you doing to overcome these hindrances?
- Who are the people you must separate from to fulfil your divinely assigned roles?

- Who are the people you must maintain contact with to fulfil your divinely assigned roles?
- What steps are you going to take to separate yourself from people who have a negative influence and align yourself with people who have a positive influence?

PART V

At the end of this section you will have an understanding of the following:

- Those who fulfilled negative roles in destiny
- The role of the Enemy in fulfilling divinely assigned roles
- The benefits of walking in divinely assigned roles
- The consequences of not walking in divinely assigned roles
- The consequences of walking in negative assigned roles

In life, God has made provision for every vision.
Every vision suffering a setback is either not from
God or the provision has not been sought for.

—OluwaFemi Lanre-Oke

Every great destiny encounters opposition. If you
don't experience opposition, then you are not doing
something great. Opposition is meant to make you
stronger, not to make you withdraw.

—OluwaFemi Lanre-Oke

15.
THOSE WHO FULFILLED NEGATIVE ROLES IN DESTINY

People like Pharaoh and Judas Iscariot are examples of men who played negative roles. They also suffered the consequences. You can choose not to play a negative role in life by deliberately choosing to love rather than hate, backbite, and gossip.

The end of Judas Iscariot was terrible. Likewise, all the soldiers in Pharaoh's army were drowned in the Red Sea. He lost his prince and suffered greatly from the plagues God sent to him. 'And Pharaoh rose up in the night, he, and all his servants, and all the Egyptians; and there was a great cry in Egypt; for there was not a house where there was not one dead' (Exod. 12:30). If you keep acting negative roles, destroying others, seeking their downfall, criticizing them, and giving bad impressions about them, you will surely suffer the consequences.

You can choose not to act a negative role by being positive and using your abilities, gifts, and potential as opportunities to lift others.

16.
THE ROLE OF THE ENEMY IN FULFILLING DIVINELY ASSIGNED ROLES

The Enemy has critical roles to play in the fulfilment of your life goals. If God had eliminated all your enemies, contrary to what may be your opinion, you wouldn't have got to where you are today. If all enemies were eliminated, hardly a person on earth would fulfil their destiny. Everybody would be too relaxed.

By divine ordinance, the Enemy has the privilege of accessing the revelation of what you are to become on earth. This is not because the Enemy is so strong that he can decode the details of your destiny. It is because God has given the Enemy proxy into the journey of your life. The Enemy has a role to play in bringing your destiny to pass. God has His way of making the Enemy work for you. An example is the case of Moses:

And there went a man of the house of Levi, and took to wife a daughter of Levi. And the woman conceived, and bare a son: and when she saw him that he was a goodly child, she hid him three months. And when she could not longer hide him, she took for him an ark of bulrushes, and daubed it with slime and with pitch, and put the child therein; and she laid it in the flags by the river's brink. And his sister stood afar off, to wit what would be done to him. And the daughter of Pharaoh came down to wash herself at the river; and her maidens walked along by the river's side; and when she saw the ark among the flags, she sent her maid to fetch it. And when she had opened it, she saw the child: and, behold, the babe wept. And she had compassion on him, and said, This is one of the Hebrews' children. Then said his sister to Pharaoh's daughter, Shall I go and call to thee a nurse of the Hebrew women, that she may nurse the child for thee? And Pharaoh's daughter said to her, Go. And the maid went and called the child's mother. And Pharaoh's daughter said unto her, Take this child away, and nurse it for me, and I will give thee thy wages. And the women took the child, and nursed it. And the child grew, and she brought him unto Pharaoh's daughter, and he became her son. And she called his name Moses: and she said, Because I drew him out of the water. (Exod. 2:1–10)

Earlier, before the birth of Moses, Pharaoh decreed that all male children born to the Hebrew women be killed or thrown into the river (Exod. 1:8–22). This was the law, and anyone found violating it would be prosecuted.

God arranged things so that those who intended to kill Moses were actually the ones who took care of him, fed him, clothed him, and sent him to school until the appointed time when the Father sent him on the assignment for which He had created him. Moses was the major reason Pharaoh wanted all male children killed, and yet Pharaoh was the one God chose to nurture Moses till the appointed time.

Many Christians are more fervent for the Lord because of their consciousness of enemies. Others would not have known the Lord except for the pursuit of the wicked against their lives.

The presence of the Enemy's attacks has kept many Christians on their toes, rather than enabling them to experience a complacent rest. Christians have become heroes and champions in faith because their enemies never gave them breathing space. Many heroes would have been unknown but for attacks from the Enemy, which kept them moving. True, some fell victim to their enemies and became casualties on the pathway to destiny. They fell and could not rise because they didn't maximize the opportunities God made available for them. But others were felled by the Enemy, got back on their feet, and continued on for the Lord.

You cannot ignore the place of the Enemy in your destiny. Paul confessed that the Devil hindered him from coming to check the flock of God; nevertheless, he fulfilled his destiny. You will fulfil yours. If Paul had not been imprisoned, he probably would not have written two-thirds of the New Testament. He would have been very busy travelling from one mission station to another. But God, who knows all things, knew that divine revelation might not become a reality if Paul was not provided the opportunity to compose.

How do you think your enemies are helping you in achieving your God-given purpose in life?

17.
THE BENEFITS OF WALKING IN DIVINELY ASSIGNED ROLES

- You will have fulfilment in life.
- You will satisfy the purpose of creation; in other words, you will not waste creation.
- Many souls will be established in Christ.
- Your generation will be blessed because of you.
- Generations after you will benefit from your impact.
- Your reward will be great in heaven.
- God will be glorified.

18.
THE CONSEQUENCES OF NOT WALKING IN DIVINELY ASSIGNED ROLES

- Your life will be miserable on earth.
- You will become a burden and not a blessing on earth.
- You will be a waste of creation.
- You will have no tangible legacy on earth.
- You will have little or no reward in heaven.
- You will not have any fulfilment on earth.
- Generations after you will be burdened with additional responsibility.
- The Enemy will rejoice over your life.
- God will not be glorified.

19.
THE CONSEQUENCES OF WALKING IN NEGATIVE ASSIGNED ROLES

- You will not go far in life.
- You will be responsible for pulling down others.
- Your generation will curse you.
- You will leave a bad legacy on earth.
- The seed after you will partake of your foolishness.
- The heavens will close over you.
- The Enemy will make you a critical vessel.
- You will miss God and glorious eternity unless you repent, give your life to Christ, and act your God-given positive roles.

Part V Summary

- 'All things work together for good to them that love God, to them who are the called according to his purpose' (Rom. 8:28).

- Whatever we make happen to others, God makes happen to us.
- We can determine if we walk in the blessings of God or in His curse.
- God's blessings are available to those who believe and walk in obedience to His counsel.
- God's curse and judgment await those who walk contrary to His will.

Part V Questions

- If you were to be rewarded for all your obedience to God's will, how would you rate yourself? Pick your place on a scale from zero to 100 per cent.
- Can you link the contribution of the Enemy to any progress in your life?
- Mention one consequence of walking in negative assigned roles.

PART VI

This section exposes you to examples of people who played critical roles in destiny. Their labour has really counted in the world. They walked in their divinely assigned roles.

- Science: Albert Einstein
- Ministry: Joseph Ayodele Babalola
- Politics: Nelson Rolihlahla Dalibhunga Mandela
- Family: Susanna Wesley – Mother of Methodism
- Sports: Taribo West
- *You* are next

Life is not a goblet to be drained, it is a measure to be filled.

—George T. Wilson

All things of this world are nothing, unless they have reference to the next.

—Spanish proverb

He only is ruined who is a bankrupt in hope, and has forgotten how to make an effort.

—The Consolidated Encyclopedic Library

The great end of life is not knowledge but action.

— Thomas Henry Huxley

The greatest difference between men is the ability to see and to act.

—OluwaFemi Lanre Oke

There is no surer way along the road to success than to follow in the footstep of those who have reached it.

—Sidney Bremer

20.
SCIENCE

ALBERT EINSTEIN (1879–1955)

by Oren Jack Turner

Born in Germany; Ulm, Wurttemberg on the 14th of March, 1879, **Albert Einstein** began schooling at the Luitpold Gymnasium, moved on to Aaru, Switzeland, then on to Swiss Federal Polytechnic in Zurich where he trained as a teacher in Physics and Mathematics. Furthering his education, he obtained his doctorate degree in 1905 and accepted a position as technical assistant in the Swiss Patent Office after acquiring Swiss citizenship.

Much of the works for which Albert Einstein is known for was produced during his stay at the patent office. In 1908, he was appointed 'privatdozent' in Bern; a Professor extraordinary at Zurich in 1909; a Professor of Theoretical physics at Prague in 1911; Director of Kaiser Wilhelm Physical Institute at the University of Berlin 1914. Other significant appointments and events in his life includes; Albert Einstein gained German citizenship in 1914 but for political reasons renounced the citizenship in 1933and moved to America to become a professor of theoretical physics at Princeton, he became a United States citizen in 1940 and retired in 1945

As a leading figure in the World Government Movement, he made enormous contributions after the 2nd World War. He went on to establish the Hebrew University of Jerusalem in collaboration with Dr. Chaim Weizmann after declining the offer of the presidency of the State of Israel.

Albert Einstein showed the determination to solve problems of physics after having a clear view of such problems. He had the ability to visualize the most important stages on the way to his objectives and always had a strategy of his own. His major achievements were just stepping stones to his next level of advancement.

Going a little deeper into his life work; Einstein at the start of his scientific work realize the inadequacies of the Newtonian mechanics, his attempt to reconcile the laws of mechanics and electromagnetic field brought about his special theory of relativity. His explanation of the Brownian movement of molecules came after he dealt with the problems of statistical mechanics and quantum theory. Furthermore, the foundation he laid for the photon theory of light stemmed from his investigation of the thermal properties of light with a low radiation density.

Among other numerous achievements, Einstein in his early days in Berlin, worked on the theory of gravitation, published his paper on general theory of relativity in 1916 and contributed to the theory of radiation and statistical mechanics. He embarked on the construction of the unified field theories in the1920s. He worked on many more theories.

Even after his retirement, Einstein continued to work on his projects. Einstein's research which is well chronicled include: *Special Theory of Relativity* (1905), *Relativity General Theory of Relativity* (1916), *Investigations on Theory of Brownian Movement* (1926), and *The Evolution of Physics* (1938). His non-scientific works among others include; About *Zionism* (1930), *Why War?* (1933), *My Philosophy* (1934), and *Out of My Later Years* (1950)

He received honorary doctorate degrees in medicine, science, philosophy form many American and European universities. In the 1920s, he was in Europe, America, the Far East for lectures and gained numerous awards for his work

Einstein's gifts resulted in his dwelling much in intellectual solitude. For relaxation, music played as an important part in his life. He was married to Mileva Maric in 1903, with two sons and a daughter; his first marriage was dissolved in 1919, but he married his cousin, Elsa Löwenthal in the same year, who died in 1936. He died on April 18, 1955, at Princeton, New Jersey.

From *Nobel Lectures, Physics 1901–1921*, Elsevier Publishing Company, Amsterdam, 1967.

From *Nobel Lectures, Physics 1901–1921*, Elsevier Publishing Company, Amsterdam, 1967.

21.
MINISTRY

JOSEPH AYODELE BABALOLA (1904–1959)

The story of Apostle Joseph Ayodele Babalola has been summed up in the words of Prof. Saburi Biobaku in this way: 'Great men appear now and again to help shape the course of human history. The history of their lives does not of itself amount to the totality of the history of man. It nevertheless serves to illuminate that history and unravel the course of human events.' Indeed the life and work of this great man of God, and in particular his unprecedented Oke-Oye Revival, which gave birth to the now known Christ Apostolic Church (CAC), should be studied and reflected upon.

Babalola was born on 25 April 1904 to David Rotimi and Marta Talabi, who were members of the Anglican church. The mysteries surrounding his birth, according to Pastor Medayese in his book *Itan Igbe dide Woli Ayo Babalola*, included the explosion of a strange and mighty object that shook the clouds. He was raised at Odo-Owa in Ilofa, a town not too far from Ilorin, Kwara State, Nigeria. His father was the church father of the CMS church in the town.

Young Babalola started school at Ilofa after he was taken by his brother, M. O. Rotimi, to Osogbo. He went as far as standard five at the All Saints' School in Osogbo, then quit and decided to become a motor mechanic apprentice. Not long after, he joined the public works department. As a steamroller driver, he was among the workers who constructed the road from Igbara-Oke to Ilesa.

Just like the Old Testament prophets, Babalola was called by God into the prophetic office to stand before men. His was a specific and personal call. It started as strange experiences on a night in September 1928, when he suddenly became restless and couldn't sleep. This state continued for a week without an indication of its cause. These experiences climaxed on a day when he was working as usual on the Ilesa–Igbara Oke road; the steamroller's engine stopped working suddenly, to his amazement. Seeing no visible problem, Babalola became confused. While he was in this state, a great voice, 'like the sound of many waters', called him thrice. The voice clearly told him that he would die if he refused to yield to the divine call to go into the world and preach.

Babalola, who like many biblical prophets did not want to yield, only gave in to the call after he had received the assurance of divine guidance. Yielding to the call mandated him to resign his appointment at the public works department. Mr Fergusson, who was the head of his unit, tried to discourage him, but young Babalola had made up his mind to the Lord's mission.

The voice he heard initially mandated him a second time to fast for seven days. He obeyed and saw a figure of a man resembling Jesus at the end of the period. The figure spoke to him at length about his divine calling and told him of the persecutions he would face. Nonetheless, he was assured of God's protection and victory. As a symbol, a prayer handbell was given to him. He was told the sound would drive evil spirits away. He was also given a bottle called 'life-giving water' which would heal all manner of sickness. From that time forth, whenever he prayed into water, divine healing was granted to all who drank it.

Babalola was enabled to spend several weeks in prayer. He was graced to see and communicate with angels, who delivered divine instructions to him. He was forbidden to wear caps for a time, according to Elder Owoyemi Abraham of Odo-Owa. On another occasion, an angel appeared to him during a prayer session and gave him a big yam from which he was ordered to eat. He was told that God fed the whole world from that tuber. Babalola was also told that God had granted him the power to deliver those possessed by evil spirits.

He was directed to go first to Odo-Owa and start preaching. He arrived at the town in a spectacular manner on a market day, covered with palm fronds and disfigured by charcoal paints. This spectacular entry occurred in October 1928, and he was taken for a madman. He wasted no time and started preaching and prophesying immediately, warning the inhabitants of the town of impending danger should they continue in their sinful ways. His look and manner got him arrested and taken to the district officer at Ilorin for allegedly disturbing the peace of the people. The authorities discharged him when the allegations could not be substantiated.

However, the rejected Babalola was quickly sought out when smallpox broke out in the town. He prayed for the victims, and they were all healed.

Pa David Rotimi, Babalola's father, had been instrumental in the establishment of a CMS church in Odo-Owa. Babalola organized regular prayer meetings in this church, which many people attended because of the miracles God performed through him. Among the regulars was Isaiah Oluyemi, who later saw the wrath of Bishop Smith of Ilorin diocese. Information reached the bishop that almost all members of the CMS church in Ilofa were seeing visions, speaking in tongues, and praying vigorously. Babalola and the visionaries were allegedly ordered by Bishop Smith to leave the church, but Babalola did not leave the town until June 1930.

On the invitation of Elder Daniel Ajibola, who was a member of the Faith Tabernacle Congregation, Babalola went to Lagos and was introduced to Pastor D. O. Odubanjo, one of the leaders of the church. The president of the Faith Tabernacle, Senior Pastor Esinsinade, listened to the details of Babalola's call and ministry, and together with other ministers of the Faith Tabernacle received him warmly into their midst.

Babalola had not yet been baptized by immersion. He was baptized by Pastor Esinsinade in the lagoon at the back of the Faith Tabernacle Church after stating a clear emphasis on the need to be baptized by immersion. He left for Odo-Owa a few days after the baptism.

The news of his conversion to the Faith Tabernacle spread and reached Pastor K. P. Titus, who was a teacher and preacher at the Sudan Interior Mission, which was thriving in Yagaa at that time. He then invited Prophet Babalola for a revival service. While in Yagba, Babalola performed mighty works of healing which led to the conversion of a lot of Muslims and Christians as well as other traditionalists.

Balalola did not use the revivals to establish a new Christian organization. Instead he declared to his followers that he was registered with the Faith Tabernacle which had baptized him. He persuaded them to become members of the same. In order to ensure the smooth conversion of his followers, he went to Lagos to confer with the leaders about the doctrines and administration of the church.

At the time, however, there was controversy among the leaders of the Faith Tabernacle over some doctrines, including the use of Western and traditional drugs versus divine healing, and about polygamy, among others. These were to be discussed and agreed upon to forestall an impending split in the church. A meeting was scheduled for 9 and 10 July 1930 in Ilesha, following the precedent set by councils held by the apostles in the scriptures.

The council met. They discussed the first of the twenty-four issues tabled, the issue of the validity of the baptism administered to a man with many wives. Then a mighty revival broke forth. The revival resulted after Babalola raised a dead child back to life and the mother went around spreading the news. The news attracted a great number of people to Oke-Oye to see the prophet. Many who were afflicted with diseases came and were healed. Indeed many mighty works were done through the use of the prayer bell and the consumption of consecrated water from a stream called Omi Ayo (Stream of Joy).

Again, thousands of people – traditional, Muslim, and Christian from many denominations – converted to the Faith Tabernacle. Space in the church halls was booked up to the extent that revival meetings had to be moved to an open field. People from all over attended. Daily, there were records of healings, deliverances, and blessings. It was testified that within three weeks, Babalola cured about one hundred lepers, sixty blind people, and fifty lame persons. Patients at the hospital in Ilesha abandoned their beds to seek healing from Babalola.

At one point it was recorded that schools belonging to the Wesleyan and Anglican churches closed down due to having insufficient funds to pay their teachers after losing majority of their members to the revival.

The assistant district officer in Ilesha visited the revival in 1930. He wrote that he saw a crowd of the lame and blind, but alluded to the fact that the whole affair was orderly. Others testified that women were delivered of long overdue pregnancies, barren women were made fruitful, the blind saw, the dumb spoke, lunacy was cured, witches confessed, and demon-possessed people were delivered.

Following this great revival, Ayo Babalola received a revelation to burn to the ground a big tree in front of King Owa's palace. This tree was believed to be the meeting point for witches and wizards. The people thought that such a move would result in Bablola's immediate death because he would arouse the anger of the old gods. To their amazement, the prophet not only lived, he waxed stronger in the Lord's work. This led Owa of Ilesha and other important personalities to fear and respect the prophet.

The waves of Babalola's revival spread all around to Ibadan, Ijebu, Lagos, and Abeokuta. Indeed, it can be said that no greater revival preceded his. It is popularly held in the Christ Apostolic Church (CAC) that at one revival meeting, attendance rose to about forty thousand. Great men of faith came as disciples to Babalola, such as Daniel Orekoya, Peter Olatunji, and Omotunde, drew inspiration from Babalola. Ibadan experienced a great revival through

Orekoya at Oke-Bola, where he reportedly raised a dead pregnant woman.

Babalola moved on to other parts of the country by the direction of the Holy Spirit, spreading the same glad tidings and great revivals. It was recorded that people turned out at each meeting to hear him preach and see miracles. He went to Offa in Kwara state, but the Muslims incited the community against him, and he had to leave to avoid bloodshed.

He went on to Usi, the Efon-Alaaye, both in Ekitiland, and he received a warm reception. In fact, it was reported that an entire building was provided for his comfort and that of his people in Efon Alaaye. He asked the oba of the town to provide an open space for prayer. He chose a large space outside town which was traditionally known as the habitation of evil spirits – the forbidden forest. The man of God, regardless of the king's efforts to dissuade him, entered, cleared the bush, and consecrated it as a prayer ground. No harm came to them. This brought a large number of the inhabitants of the land to the faith he professed.

Babalola's evangelistic success in Efon-Alaaye was so remarkable that some white pastors, including Archdeacon H. Dallimore from Ado-Ekiti and the Ogbomosho Baptist Seminary, came for themselves to see the 'wonder – working prophet'. The conversion of the kings of Efon and Aramoko, who were baptized with the names Solomon Aladejare Agunsooye and Hezekaiah Adeoye respectively, spread the news of the revival at Efon to other parts of Ekitiland. Babalola further visited other towns in the present Ondo state, such as Owo, Ikarem, and Oka.

Babalola was, however, arrested and sentenced to jail in Benin City in March 1932 for preaching against witches, a practice which had caused some trouble in Otuo in the old Bendel state. After serving the jail sentence, he returned to his assignment.

His assignment expanded when Mr Cyprian E. Ufon came from Creek Town in Calabar to ask for Babalola's help. He had heard about Babalola and his works and wanted him to preach in Creek Town. The prophet followed Ufon to Creek Town after seeking divine direction and embarked upon a very successful campaign.

From Creek Town, Babalola visited Duke Town and a plantation where a national church existed at the time. Members of this church received the gift of the Holy Spirit as Babalola was preaching to them and were baptized. When the prophet returned from the Calabar area, he settled down for a while, and in 1935 he married Dorcas.

Babalola, accompanied by Evangelist Timothy Bababusuyi, went to the Gold Coast the next year and had a successful ministry, after which he returned to Nigeria. Upon arrival, he was recognized by some people who had been at his great revival in Ilesha.

Prophet Joseph Ayo Babalola's evangelism was not without its waves of persecution. Mission churches became jealous and hostile because they lost members, who constituted the main converts of the Faith Tabernacle. Rumours were raised and spread about the revival movement, calling it lawless. Even the Nigerian government was put on alert about his activities.

The Faith Tabernacle, an offshoot of the American Faith Tabernacle, had their own crises and called their leaders abroad to come home to their rescue. But the call was turned down. The foreign leaders would not have any part in the movement, saying it was against their principles. The relationship between the two churches was terminated following the marital challenges of Pastor Clark, the leader of the American group.

Though the Nigerian Faith Tabernacle had disappointing relations with these foreign groups, further efforts to seek affiliation with a foreign body stemmed from a letter written by D. O. Odubanjo to Pastor D. P. Williams of the Apostolic Church of Great Britain in March 1931. The letter emphasized that 'the Nigerian government fear the European missionaries and dare not trouble their native converts. Although often, they have been ill-treated by government officers'.

A formal request was sent for missionaries to strengthen the Nigerian Faith Tabernacle. This led to the church's migration to the British Apostolic Church. As a consequence, the Faith Tabernacle changed its name to the Apostolic Church.

Doctrinal differences led to a great controversy among the leading members. The controversy unfortunately proved unresolvable and led to a split of the Apostolic Church. A faction of the church stayed at Oke-Oye and retained the name 'the Apostolic Church', while the larger faction, with Prophet Joseph Babalola as a leader, became the Christ Apostolic Church.

The church went through many names before May 1943, but it was finally registered. Today, it controls over five thousand assemblies and reputedly is one of the most popular Christian organizations in Nigeria.

Babalola was a spiritually gifted individual who was genuinely dissatisfied with the increasing materialistic and sinful existence into which he believed the Yoruba in particular and Nigeria in general were being plunged as Western civilization influence on society grew.

The C.A.C. believes that the spiritual power bestowed on Babalola placed him on an equal level with biblical apostles like Peter, Paul, and others who were sent out with the authority and in the name of Jesus.

Joseph Ayo Babalola slept in the Lord in 1959.

22.
POLITICS

NELSON ROLIHLAHLA DALIBHUNGA MANDELA (1918–2013)

Credit: "South Africa The Good News";
www.sagoodnews.co.za

Born 18 July 1918, Nelson Mandela (Nelson Rolihlahla Dalibhunga Mandela) was of royal birth. He was born near Umtata in Transkei on the Eastern Cape of South Africa. His father, who was the principal councillor to the acting paramount chief of Thembuland, died in 1927, and Rolihlahla became the chief's foster son. This ensured that he was groomed to become a ruling member of his tribe.

The South African system of segregation and oppression, apartheid, was familiar to Mandela from an early age. The injustices he witnessed and the cases brought before the chief's court had a great effect on him as a young man, and he decided to become a lawyer. He obtained his law degree from the University of South Africa after starting his studies at the Fort Hare University. He was expelled from there in 1940 for leading a strike with his friend Oliver Tambo. The law degree he eventually obtained was by correspondence.

Mandela joined the African National Congress (ANC) in1942 as his debut in politics. The ANC then was a black nationalist movement. In 1944, together with Tambo, he helped form the ANC Youth League, a group grounded in the principle of national self-determination. They called for radical African nationalism. In 1947, he was elected the secretary of the league, which came to dominate the ANC by 1948.

In the 1948 elections, which saw the victory of the National Party, apartheid discrimination against black South Africans was written into law. This was because the National Party was dominated by white settlers known as Afrikaners.

In 1949, Mandela was elected to the National Executive Committee (NEC) of the ANC, and named president of the Youth League the following year.

In 1952, after travelling throughout South Africa recruiting volunteers for a major civil disobedience campaign, he got arrested and convicted for organizing the campaign, and was confined in Johannesburg for six months. He passed his bar exam during this time and founded South Africa's first black law partnership with his friend Tambo. Throughout the 1950s, he was the victim of many forms of repression – arrested, imprisoned, and banned.

He was one of those accused in the Treason Trial in 1956–1961, at a huge cost to his legal practice and political work. In fact, following the Sharpeville Massacre in 1960, the ANC was outlawed. Quitting in 1961, Mandela went underground and formed what was called the Umkhonto we Sizwe, the ANC's military wing. He became the unit's commander-in-chief.

He left the country unlawfully, travelling for several months in 1962. Upon his return, he was charged with illegal exit from the country and incitement to strike. He was sentenced to five years in prison with hard labour.

In 1963, several leaders of the ANC and its military arm were arrested, and Mandela was brought to stand trial with them for scheming to overthrow the government by violence. On 12 June 1964, eight of the accused ANC leaders, including Mandela, were sentenced to life in prison. Mandela was sent to the notorious Robben Island Prison, a maximum-security jail near Cape Town.

It was during his years in prison that Mandela's reputation as South Africa's most significant black leader, as well as a symbol for equal rights, justice, and resistance against apartheid, grew. While in prison, Mandela refused to compromise his political beliefs in order to obtain his freedom. He stated that 'only free men can negotiate. Prisoners cannot enter into contracts'.

In April 1982, Mandela was moved to Pollsmoor Prison on the mainland. December 1988 saw his transfer to another prison, Victor Verster Prison. He was eventually released in February 1990, after nearly twenty-seven years in prison.

After his release, Mandela resumed his work, which was to dismantle the system of apartheid. The year 1991 witnessed the first national conference of the ANC in South Africa. Mandela was elected president and his ever-committed friend and colleague, Oliver Tambo, became the ANC's national chairperson. Mandela played a pivotal role in the subsequent negotiations that ended apartheid in his country.

Other achievements of Nelson Mandela include:

- He and South African President F.W Klerk shared the 1993 Nobel Peace Prize, which he accepted on behalf of all South Africans who had suffered and sacrificed to bring peace to the land.
- In May 1994, at 75 years of age, he won the first all-race election in South Africa and became the first elected black president.

- On 10 December 1996, he signed the country's new constitution, which included extensive human rights and anti-discrimination guarantees.

Having achieved all this, Nelson Mandela stepped down as president in 1999 and voiced his intention to enjoy the peace and freedom it had taken a lifetime to achieve. He returned to his native village and spent time with his third wife and grandchildren, writing as many memoirs as he could.

Though he intended to enjoy peace and freedom, his retirement period was a busy one for him. He frequently travelled overseas and mediated peace efforts in many nations, such as Burundi. He was most respected in South Africa for the major role he played in transforming the government from a dark, gloomy apartheid regime to a free and fair democracy.

Nelson Mandela died on 5 December 2013 at the ripe age of 95.

23.
FAMILY

SUSANNA WESLEY – MOTHER OF METHODISM

by Ronald M. Higashi

Help me, Lord, to remember that religion is not to be confined to the church ... nor exercised only in prayer and meditation, but that every where I am in Thy Presence.
—Susanna Wesley

Susanna Wesley
Image by: GBGM Administration

It is only fitting that, on Mother's Day, we honour and remember **Susanna Wesley,** the mother of John and Charles Wesley, founders of Methodism.

Susanna Annesley Wesley was the youngest of twenty-five children born to the family of Dr. Samuel Annesley, a well-known minister of the time. Susanna Wesley and her husband, Samuel, also a minister, had nineteen children in the first nineteen years of marriage. Ten lived past infancy.

Susanna Wesley was an extraordinary woman devoted to God and her family. Her faith in God allowed the family to survive and face the grief, hardship, and poverty that filled their lives. Her conquering of adversity is still a great inspiration to us all today.

Susanna Wesley drew her inner strength from her belief in God. She took it beyond the church and integrated it into her daily family life.

Her husband, Samuel Wesley, was a controversial religious and political figure of the time. The Wesley family was subject to much ridicule and in some instances the target of malicious acts, because they were known as 'dissenters' – people who disagreed with the king's and the church's politics and failure to care for those in need. Their children were mocked, the family crops destroyed, and it was suspected that the rectory was burned due to his beliefs. Samuel himself was committed to 'debtors' prison' for a period of time by a parishioner demanding payment.

During these the very harshest of times, Susanna was committed to caring for her family the best way possible. Although resources were very limited, she started a daily school for her children. She said her primary purpose was the spiritual development of her children and 'the saving of their souls.' Academic education was important but never took priority over instruction in God's Word.

As a caring mother, she set aside a 'special time' with each of her children. Those were 'bonding' times when each child was free to discuss whatever he or she wanted, and she would offer her 'motherly advice and consul.' These weekly private appointments for encouragement could be called 'quality time' today. She developed faith, fear of God, and resiliency in each child.

This bond and sense of faith Susanna established with each of her children empowered John and Charles Wesley to go forth in confidence, their character strengthened by their mother.

Samuel Wesley, her husband, wrote this to his children, 'With deep admiration, you know what you owe to one of the best of mothers ... above all (for) the wholesome and sweet motherly advice and counsel which she has often given you to fear God …'

So profound was the influence of Susanna Wesley upon her son, John Wesley, that she has been called 'The Mother of Methodism'.

24.
SPORTS

TARIBO WEST (1974–)

Taribo West was born 26 March 1974, in Lagos, Nigeria. He is a Nigerian football defender, whose football career ended after he was released by English Championship team Plymouth Argyle on 6 October 2005.

West has had a successful career, playing for AJ Auxerre, Inter Milan, A. C. Milan, Derby County, FC Kaiserslautern, FK Partizan, Al-Arabi, Bolton Wanderers, and Plymouth Argyle. He has been capped forty-one times by the Nigerian national team and played in the 1998 and 2002 World Cups. He was also a member of the Nigerian team that won the gold medal at the 1996 Summer Olympics in Atlanta, Georgia. West is also known for the various unusual and colourful hairstyles that he has sported over the years.

Having left football, he is currently a pastor in Lagos, Nigeria.

In August 2005, Derby County fans sent shirts to Taribo West's hometown in Africa campaign, backed by BBC Radio Derby.

25.
YOU ARE NEXT

Then the king Ahasuerus said unto Esther the queen and to Mordecai the Jew, Behold, I have given Esther the house of Haman, and him they have hanged upon the gallows, because he laid his hand upon the Jews. Write ye also for the Jews, as it liketh you, in the king's name, and seal it with the king's ring: for the writing which is written in the king's name, and sealed with the king's ring, may no man reverse. (Esther 8:7–8)

Today, Jesus, the King of Kings, is giving you permission to write your own story as it pleases you. You can follow this format in prayerfully writing your own epitaph:

Name:

Duration of your story: Year _____ to 20__

What you want to be remembered for:

    Career Achievements

Calling or Spiritual Achievements

Financial Achievements

Other Achievements

Part VI Summary

- No one is exempt from the game of destiny.
- We are not equal, but we are all born to be great.
- How great God will make you is dependent on how much you are willing to cooperate with His will for your life and to follow Him.
- No one is a failure in life except a person who chooses to be one.
- Diligence is a key factor and price in the climb to greatness.
- Of 848 great men examined on earth, 807 were ardent followers of Christ.
- Nothing on earth is permitted to hinder a man who in himself is determined to follow Christ and succeed.

Part VI Questions

- What would you say is an excuse for not doing God's will? (Should you have any?)
- How must you live your life now to succeed as you follow Christ?

CONCLUSION

This book has been written with divine inspiration to impart that inspiration into your life and ignite your passion to use your innate potential on earth. No matter how old you are, you can begin to make your mark and create your impact.

There is something critical about you in the mind of God. That is why He created you. There is nothing about you that is accidental. God made you because of something in His heart. He wants you to translate that meaning and make it happen. Everything happening to you is because of what you are created to be.

The Enemy is interested in your life and destiny because of the glory attached to it. You will, however, not make that glory happen if you continue to jump from one place to the other. You must devote time to seek the presence of the almighty God to reveal His mind about you. It is my prayer for you that, as you find time to seek Him, you will find Him.

Many prayers have gone ahead of this book so that it may serve the purpose for which it was written. I believe your contact with this book is not accidental; there may be one or two things the Lord desires you to learn from it. And if this book has enabled you or further enabled you to walk in the divinely assigned role God has for you, then the purpose for which it was written is fulfilled.

If you think you have been blessed by your copy of this book, then buy one for a friend. We could have a better world if we do what He has sent us to do. I believe that, if it doesn't happen on this earth, we will one day meet in the Master's kingdom, where we will all give an account of what we have done in the flesh while on earth.

I believe strongly that you will have no excuse for not fulfilling your destiny.

My prayers are with you.

HYMN

When Jesus Comes
Fanny J. Cosby (1820–1915)

1. When Jesus comes to reward His servants
   Whether it be noon or night
   Faithfull to Him will He find us watching
   With our lamps all trimmed and bright?

   Oh can we say we are ready brother?
   Ready for the soul's bright home?
   Say will He find you and me still watching?
   Watching, watching when the Lord shall come

2. If at the dawn of the early morning
   He shall call us one by one
   When to the Lord we restore our talents
   Will He answer us well done?

3. Have we been true to the truth He left us?
   Do we seek to do our best?

If in heart there is not condemn us
We shall have a glorious rest.

4. Blessed are those whom the Lord finds watching
   In His glory they shall share
   If He shall come at dawn or mid night
   Will He find us watching there?

ABOUT THE AUTHOR

OluwaFemi Lanre-Oke is a teacher of God's Word, a pastor, a bestselling author, and a destiny coach and speaker. He travels extensively as a consultant for government organizations, civic organizations, and the body of Christ.

He is the president and founder of Jesus Praise Evangelical Ministries International, an all-encompassing network of ministries headquartered in Oyo State, Nigeria.

He is the president and facilitator of the renowned Kingdom Leadership College, with a focus on leadership and character development.

He is a regular national daily columnist and host of the radio programme *His Kingdom Hour.* He earned a master's degree in information technology from Ladoke Akintola University of Technology, Ogbomoso, Oyo State, Nigeria.

Lanre-Oke is married to Olubusola. They are both ministers of the gospel and are blessed with children.

You can contact OluwaFemi Lanre-Oke:
Phone: +2348030752799, +2348053695097
E-mail: femi_lanre01@yahoo.co.uk
www.jpeministries.org

ABOUT THE BOOK

God's way is unique. Not every labour will count on the last day.

Many will say to me in that day, Lord, Lord, have we not prophesied in thy name? And in thy name have cast out devils? And in thy name done many wonderful works? And then will I profess unto them, I never knew you: depart from me, ye that work iniquity. (Matt. 7:22–23)

On that day, only labourers who are in alignment with God's purpose and counsel will count.
   In this book, you will learn:

- How to recognize labour that will count
- God's provisions for fulfilling your divinely assigned roles
- The Enemy's role in fulfilling your divinely assigned roles

- How to discover and fulfil your purpose
- The different kinds of roles

By holding this book, you are being moved by God into a new era of destiny fulfilment. After you read this book, you will be the next testimony.

Printed in the United States
By Bookmasters